CALLING MY SPIRIT BACK

ELAINE ALEC

tellwell

Tellwell Talent
www.tellwell.ca

ISBN
978-0-2288-3069-6 (Paperback)
978-0-2288-3070-2 (eBook)

INTRODUCTION

There are many forces that can damage a community and the people within it, especially those who have become marginalized by forces beyond their control. But Indigenous peoples have always carried the knowledge necessary to heal. When our people heal, our families heal, our communities heal, and our land will heal. You cannot have one without the others.

The stories in this book are teachings, prophesies and protocols shared throughout the years by elders, Indigenous-language speakers, medicine people and helpers. They have been the foundation of individual healing and of learning self-love. They teach us how to make good decisions for ourselves and for all other aspects of our lives, including our family, our community and our workplace.

Before contact with settlers, our people were sent on the land when they were young to gather as much experience and knowledge as they could, and when they returned they would contribute what they had learned.

I am Syilx and Secwepemc from the Southern Interior of British Columbia. I spent most of my life in Penticton, which is my mother's territory, the Syilx Nation, also known as the Okanagan Nation. Our nation extends across the Canada-United States border into Washington State, and although many of my teachings come from this place, they also intertwine with Indigenous knowledge shared through ceremony from many other nations across North America.

People from all backgrounds have embraced concepts from other parts of the world that promote self-love, healing and well-being through practices of discipline and meditation, but very little has been shared outside Indigenous communities about our systems and how they take care of our health and spiritual needs.

Indigenous peoples continue to remember and reclaim our ancestral wisdom and our responsibilities, which ensure each living being is taught to exist in balance with all creation.

These stories are a way of sharing knowledge and love, of promoting healing and unity. This same knowledge and process is utilized to make important decisions, govern and plan within our communities.

This way of being teaches us ways to cultivate safe spaces for ourselves and others through understanding of self, love-based practice, patience and discipline. This philosophy is shared at the end of the book, but in order to get there you have to go through the rest. Some of it might not be easy to read, but the stories of our past, of our individual experiences, have to be exposed to the light so that we can heal collectively.

In order to know where we're going, we have to know where we've been.

When I was twenty-nine years old, I sat in a circle with a woman from a northern Cree nation in Alberta and she told us that before we are human beings, we are light.

When we are light, we see everything. We see the past and we see the future. We see how everything will happen in our lives, and we know what our purpose is.

As light, we pick our parents before we are born. We pick them and everyone that comes into our lives. We pick our experiences and everything that happens to us. We know the path we pick will make us grow and contribute to who we are as human beings in order to live our purpose.

Some individuals remember everything they knew as light. Most of us forget what our purpose is, and it makes our time on Earth a struggle until we find our way back to our purpose, if we ever do.

I have struggled in this human life to understand and accept this teaching, but it has become one of the reasons I continue to move forward. I have never considered myself a survivor. I grew up as the oldest child of an alcoholic mother and I had a father who did not stay in one place.

I was sexually abused as a child from the ages of four to ten. Not just by one individual in my community, but by many. My mom would leave us with babysitters or have them come over so she could go out to drink. When we got older, she would have parties and people would come in and out of our house at all hours of the night.

At six years old, I would make a bed in my closet for myself and my little sister so we had a place to sleep where no one would bother us. We witnessed many kinds of abuse, but it was normal to me and everyone around me. We all knew what was happening, but we didn't talk about it.

I started smoking at ten, and I had my first drink at twelve. I ran away from home and hitchhiked across British Columbia. I became pregnant at seventeen and had my son Kyle when I was eighteen.

My dad was a quadriplegic who passed away when I was pregnant at eighteen. My mom had a massive stroke that left her unable to speak or walk when I was nineteen. At twenty-one, I developed rheumatoid arthritis and fibromyalgia and could barely walk down the stairs or brush my hair. My rheumatologist told me I would be in a wheelchair by the time I was thirty.

I attempted suicide at twenty-two. I popped pills. I was a raging alcoholic, and I abused my partners. I ended up in the back of cop cars after getting into fistfights in the middle of the street. I lived in poverty and hoped that no one knew how bad it was. There were times I didn't think I was that bad. At least I wasn't as bad as some people I knew.

There were weeks when all I had was flour and baking powder, so I made oven bread. Sometimes I didn't have money to pay bills, so we didn't have power. I thought it was okay because no one knew how bad it was and at least we had a house to live in.

My trauma created chaos and lived in my spirit and body. It affected the way I did things throughout my life; it made my decisions and caused me physical and mental anguish, contributing to my alcoholism, anger and self-inflicted pain. That was my life, and it was all I knew.

I didn't see anything beyond the moment I was in. I never believed I could have a life without the anger and chaos. I had a

Grade-9 education and lived in debt and poverty. It was a long road, but I now find myself in a place I never dreamed I would be.

I am wrapping up my three-year term as the Union of British Columbia Indian Chiefs Women's Representative. I am a partner in my own company, Alderhill Planning Inc., with Chief Chris Derickson and Jessie Hemphill. We are seen as leading experts in Indigenous planning and our work takes us across Canada. We have worked with over 150 Indigenous communities across the country and advise and work with both federal and provincial governments. We have grown substantially over the past four years and, besides our three partners, we now have three full-time staff and four associates.

I am married to the most brilliant and beautiful man I have ever known. Ryan grew up in Kitimat but ended up back in Secwepemc territory in Cache Creek, B.C., where he became chief for two terms. He is a marathon runner, a hunter, a berry picker, a root digger, a fisher, a thinker and a builder. I never believed I was deserving of love and happiness.

I have three children. All of them were raised in very different worlds with three very different versions of me. I would like to say I have no regrets in life and have been through only learning experiences, but I would be lying. I will always wish things had been different for my oldest. It took me twenty years to learn how to be a mom I could be proud of.

Today, I have three children who are safe, secure, healthy and loved. It was a long road of learning, of being humbled and finding ways to continue moving forward.

My story may be rooted in trauma, but it is not my only story.

2

My name is Telxnitkw. It translates into "Standing by Water." My tema gave me my name on the day I was born. My tema, or grandmother, Ellen Alec, was also known as Philomen Francois. When the missionaries came to our territories, they gave us names. In most cases, there was no rhyme or reason to how our names were chosen for us. Sometimes names were given to us and then changed by Indian agents for their own purposes and record keeping. Some nations in other territories were given names based on what they thought they heard in English, and others were given names based on what their ancestors were known for. In the Prairies, they have names like Buffalo and Eagle Speaker. Many of our ancestors were named after the missionaries and their family lines.

My tema was the daughter of Chief Francois from the Syilx Nation, who was a descendant of Soorimpt, themselves a descendant of Keltpikchenkn and Pelkamulaxw from the Syilx, Colville and Nez Perce territories. Pelkamulaxw was one of our great hereditary chiefs. He was born in the 1600s and had twenty-four wives from different nations between Southern Washington and Southern British Columbia. Our family are also descendants of Chief Joseph, who came from the Nez Perce Nation. He spent many years on the Colville Indian Reservation in Washington State before he died in 1904.

Tema was born on February 14, 1904. She grew up in Penticton, B.C. and told stories of setting up their summer camps in Oyama, B.C., where they would live, gather and fish. This area is now taken over by million-dollar lakefront properties.

My tema was married to my grandfather Jack Alec for forty-five years. He was chief of the Penticton Indian Band for twenty-four years until he passed away in 1974. They had twelve children, including my mother, Sophie Alec.

My late father was Saul "Kenzie" Basil. He was a militant and radical. He was political and outspoken. He was born to Louisa and Saul Basil of the Bonaparte Indian Band near Cache Creek, B.C. He was from the Secwepemc Nation and was chief for a short time for his people.

My dad would travel all over the country, and people would call him when they needed help to mobilize protests and blockades. He would often travel with Larry "Joe Face" Joseph and Clarence "C.D." Dennis, who were both from Vancouver Island. They were his friends and brothers, and they were all active in the Red Power Movement and leaders within their own nations.

My dad had no fear of government or authority. He was a writer and philosopher and embodied a warrior spirit until the day he died. Many of the elders who remember him still refer to him as their War Chief.

I am the second youngest of his nine children: Dawn, Teri, Shanon, Jody, D'arcy, Evelyn, me, and a brother and sister from White Swan, Washington. We have never met our brother and sister from Washington, but we were told about them at my dad's funeral, where we met our brother Jody for the first time. There could be more. My dad had two children with Sophie: my younger sister Evelyn and me. My dad later told me that he met my mom in a bar, and that I was conceived two weeks later.

I also have adopted and chosen brothers and sisters who became some of the most important people in my world. They were present during many of the most difficult moments of my young life, stuck with me through a lot of my most undesirable moments, and helped take care of me when no one else knew how bad things were.

Our communities often adopted people into our families. Formal adoption in our communities didn't mean we signed papers, it meant that individuals were introduced as family through ceremony or public acknowledgement. Informal adoptions in our communities meant that we spent so much time together that we ended up taking each other as family.

My little sister Emma-Lena was brought into our lives by a stepdad, and even though our parents didn't stay together, we still refer to her as our baby sister. My sister Wynette was adopted into our family when she was twelve years old.

My brother Jeremy was adopted through a ceremony when my mom had her first stroke. He lives in Eastern Canada, but we spent many summers travelling together to powwows across the United States. My brother Nacoma began dating my sister Evelyn when they were fourteen, and he has been my closest brother throughout the years, someone I have come to rely on. They have been the best aunties and uncles to my children.

Both of my parents went to residential schools in British Columbia. My mom went to the St. Eugene Mission in Cranbrook, and my dad went to the Kamloops Indian Residential School. I didn't know what a residential school was until I was in my late twenties.

I spent most of my early childhood with my tema on the Penticton Indian Band reserve. Back then we had approximately 150 houses on our reserve and about 250 people living in our community. My tema was my mom's mother, a devout Catholic who sang hymns in the nsyilxcen language. Growing up, many of our people referred to themselves as "Okanagan people," and our language was called "Okanagan." It wasn't until I became older that I started to refer to myself and my nation as *Syilx*, and to my language as *nsyilxcen*. Over the years, I went from calling myself an "Indian" to a "Native" to a "First Nations" to an "Aboriginal" to an "Indigenous person." As I grew, I also learned more about our nsyilxcen language and that we were more than just "Okanagan People."

My tema's singing was the first thing I heard in the morning before the sun came up. I was only four years old, yet she would share her stories with us before she sent us outside. We had to introduce ourselves to the land in our nsyilxcen name so the land would know who we were and protect us. She told us to do things a certain way, but we were never allowed to ask why.

My little sister Evelyn learned how to walk when I was three years old. My tema had two sons, the youngest of her children: my Uncle Jeff and my Uncle Louie. They told us stories about how I dragged my sister all over the place, and they worried that she would end up walking sideways forever.

At the time, Evelyn and I didn't know about residential schools. We did not know they punished our people for speaking our language and sharing our stories, so we didn't understand what a gift it was and what a rebel my tema was for telling us those stories and sharing those teachings.

Our stories tell us who we are. They tell us there was a beginning for our people, and a time before our people came to this world as human beings. These stories tell us the laws and how to govern ourselves; they tell us how to live in harmony with ourselves, our family, our community, and our land.

Our first law is to understand and live in balance with the world. Our stories are called *captikwl*, and they carry our laws through our language. One of our stories told of what our people would go through in the four stages of evolution in this human life.

The first stage of evolution involved the first people, who were born without natural instincts to survive. They were called *st'elsqilxw* ("torn from the earth *sqilxw*").

The second stage were the first thinking people, who learned the natural law in order to survive. They were called *xatmaʔsqilxw* ("in front of us *sqilxw*").

The third stage were the dreaming ones, who bound themselves together and were of the land. They were the original people who learned to live together on the land in peace. They were called *sqilxw* ("dreaming ones, bound together, of the land").

The fourth stage is where we are today: the ones who will struggle after the arrival of the newcomers. We are *ʔawtmaʔsqilxw* ("to struggle and/or come after *sqilxw*").

There are other stories our families share that remind us of our responsibilities as a family and how to behave in our community. We were told what land we were responsible for and how to care for it.

We have stories about Sen'klip. Sen'klip was a trickster. Sen'klip was Coyote. He did many things for our people and taught us many lessons. Coyote had a good side and bad side. The good side of Coyote was Sm'yawt, the mischievous side, and Sen'klip was the side used in oral teachings to reflect what is expected of a person. Coyote teachings helped us understand that there were consequences for our actions. The stories show people what not to do. My mom used to tell me Coyote was our equivalent to Jesus.

Sometimes my mom would take us for a cruise in our old brown station wagon. We would pick up my tema and just drive around. My tema would tell us stories about rocks, mountains and lakes. She would point out the places where she did things as a little girl and tell us funny stories about her and her sister Angeline.

When I stayed at my tema's house, she would let us share her bed with her at night. She would rub my back and tell me the story of Chipmunk and Owl. She used her hands to mimic Chipmunk jumping from tree branch to tree branch. She always shared the story in our language, and I could understand everything she said.

She would also tell us the story of the Four Food Chiefs and Fly, and the time Coyote lost his guts.

Sometimes she would send me outside at night. She would tell me that she had left something on the woodpile. I could never make it past the bottom porch step because I was too scared to go into the dark. Other times she would send me to the creek to jump in or wash my face. She would tell me to do little rituals when I was there, and I thought she was just telling me to go play. Sometimes she would make me pick berries or gather plants for her. I would call a taxi for her so she could go to the bank and go grocery shopping. I was her interpreter when we would do errands in town, and when she signed a cheque for cash, she wrote her name as a little wobbly "X."

My tema brought me everywhere. I listened to her beautiful language and stories. She told me to do things that didn't always make sense to me. Later, I found out she was helping me find my spirit helper. When I got older, I listened to one of my teachers talk about "rites of passage" or "coming of age." She told us that by the time we turned four years old, our grandparents would give us tasks to do, like sending us out in the dark in hopes that our spirit helper would show themselves to us.

My tema would tell me to take her to church, and to come with her to visit her friends or her sister, and we would get ready and walk down the road. I was my tema's human walking cane. When we went visiting, I only had one job: to listen. I would serve her and her friends tea and cookies and help them get up and down from their seats. I could not run around or act up or make too much noise. I was only there to serve the elders.

My mom took me to meetings where elders were talking and many band meetings where our people spoke their original language, nsyilxcen. When I was little, there were important meetings held with the elders to talk about what stories to share through books and writing. I don't know if I was at any of those meetings, but I remember one day my mom was excited because she had three books for me and my sister to share. Our elders had picked three stories, and one was "How Food Was Given" or "Four Food Chiefs." This is one of the most important stories our people share.

I've heard short versions of the story told in many ways over the years. This story has become an important guide for me. It helps me consider how I carry myself. It helps to ground me, and it is the foundation for how I make decisions.

After hearing many versions of this story over the years, this is how I share the short version of this story:

In the beginning, there were four chiefs. Chief Black Bear was the chief of all things that walked the earth and flew in the sky. Chief Bitterroot was the chief of all things that grew below ground. Chief Saskatoon Berry was the chief for all things that grew above ground. Chief Spring Salmon was chief of all things that lived in the water.

The Creator came and told the chiefs that new beings would come to live among them. They called these new beings the "People to Be." The Creator instructed the chiefs to figure out how to help the People to Be survive.

The chiefs talked to each other until one said, "This is a pitiful being. It has no fur to keep it warm. It has no claws to protect itself. It has no teeth to eat. It has no instinct to keep itself alive. How are we supposed to help this being survive?"

The chiefs thought long and hard about this before they looked at Chief Black Bear and said, "You are the eldest. What do you think we should do?"

Chief Black Bear thought for a while longer and said, "I will lay my life down for the People to Be so they will have the best chance at survival. They can have my meat, my fur, my teeth and claws. They can have whatever they need to survive."

All the chiefs said they would do the same. Before Chief Black Bear laid himself down, he said, "You must sing me back to life so that my body will always regenerate and continue to feed the people."

Chief Black Bear laid his life down and the chiefs sang their song, but Chief Black Bear did not come back to life.

All the living things came, and each sang their own song. Still, Chief Black Bear did not come back to life.

It wasn't until the last living being came and said, "Let me sing my song. I want to sing my song!"

Everyone shooed him away and said, "No one wants to hear your song. You are a pest and you eat manure. No one wants to hear your song!"

It was Fly who had come to sing. He got through the crowd to sit on Chief Black Bear's ear. Fly sang his song and only then did Chief Black Bear come back to life.

When I was told this story as a child, my teaching was to honour all the living things who gave up their life for me.

I was told to respect all life and give thanks to it. I could not do senseless things on the land or to animals. I was taught ways of fishing and gathering that honoured the life we were taking, and I was taught to always give thanks and have gratitude.

My teachers shared with me that we are born with something other living beings are not: a mind capable of memory, and intelligence to create and learn language to pass on our knowledge.

The animals are our family. They are our parents, and if we respect them we do not have to be afraid of them. When we go on the land, we introduce ourselves with our nsyilxcen name so the land will know who we are.

My family was great at teaching us about Fly in all parts of our life. They raised us to respect Fly. Fly was small and annoying, but just as important as everyone else. When people come into our lives who are Fly, we have to listen to them because they are here to teach us a lesson.

My family taught me that when people make fun of me or call me names, I'm not to take it inside of me or hold on to it. My mom would tell me that I should probably feel sorry for them, and that they were most likely hurting and that was why they were being mean.

I was always taught to think of why people behaved a certain way instead of taking it personally.

When I was little, I was told certain stories for certain teachings. As I got older, I learned more complex teachings, with more words and more ways of seeing and knowing things.

As an adult, I began to understand that each being has purpose, even a small and seemingly insignificant pest. I learned that Fly's song was just as powerful as the chief's song, and when we take the time to hear everyone's song we are so powerful we can bring back life.

Sometimes we don't think alike. We might not even like each other or agree. But it is important to listen to all views and perspectives to develop a full picture so we can make good decisions for our people.

We all have powerful prayers. We can make things happen, especially if we do them together. Great things happen if we know how to listen and learn from all peoples, teachings, beliefs and religions.

Our family was raised to be open to everyone and respect how different we are. They centred most of our learning around listening and paying attention to the world. My mom always said, "Don't just think about yourself when you talk to people." It took me a really long time to figure out what she meant.

3

When I was four years old, I already knew my mom wasn't always going to be around. I learned how to use the phone to call a taxi when my mom didn't come home. We would always end up at my tema's house. My uncle told me he always knew it was my sister and me arriving when he would hear a taxi pull into the driveway. He would look out the window and see only the cab driver, but then the back door would open up and out of the back my sister and I would climb. He would tell my tema we were there and my tema called me something in Okanagan that translated into "so smart she's scary."

We lived in a tiny old house that my grandpa built in the early 1900s. The house was at the base of a hill covered in antelope brush and grasslands. On the south side of the house was a creek. There were lilacs lined along the front and side of my tema's house.

I played at the creek, in the hills and on the clay banks. That was where the little people lived. My tema would tell us not to bother them and to be good. All the kids on the reserve knew what the little people were; we would tell stories our parents told us or ones about encounters with them. The little people were spirits that reminded us to take care of ourselves, and they were tricksters. Often you would hear adults complain about losing keys they had just put down on the table. They would blame the little people for hiding things on them.

I went for long walks that would start at the beginning of the day. I would wander around the community and find other kids, play in the creek and go fishing or visit other houses. No one locked their doors and people always shared the food they had. I remember lying in the knapweeds on the flats of our community and watching bears. They never paid attention to us and we never thought they would ever hurt us. Sometimes I would lose track of time while playing and have to run home fast before the sun went down, because nighttime was when the spirits came. My tema told us stories about Owl Woman, who would steal children who were bad or stayed out late. Owl Woman made sure kids behaved and didn't yell or make too much noise at night.

Time with my tema was the safest part of my life. She took care of us and raised us in such a wonderful way, filled with love, humour and understanding. She was a tiny and tough woman in her mid-seventies. My tema was the matriarch of the family, and my mom and uncles never challenged her. She was wise and ancient and absolute in her knowing. She loved to watch TV shows like *Dallas* and *Another World* and laugh at me and my sister who would play in front of her and act silly.

I grew up with a fairly normal life on the reserve, where dysfunction was the norm and always surrounded me. When you grow up that way, you just assume that's the way life is. Things outside of my tema's house were dark.

There were many times when I tried to turn and face my past, but I found it too painful. I stopped going to those places in my memories when I was young because I was afraid that I would go crazy. I believed if people knew what was going on in my head, they would think I was crazy.

If my mom wasn't leaving us alone at home or with my tema, she would take us with her and leave us in the vehicle outside of the bar. One time, she felt guilty, so she called one of my cousins to come and get me and my sister.

Sometimes I would get home from school or from visiting friends after school and my mom would be drunk. She would cry and tell me she thought I had left her because I hadn't come home from school right away. Other times she would get angry and tell me how I should trust no man, and that I should always take care of myself and make sure everything I ever had in my life was mine alone.

She told me stories about cheating with a married man, and that when she turned eighteen he divorced his wife to marry her. As soon as they married he began to beat her and have affairs. He expected her to have dinner ready at six p.m. sharp, and if she didn't he would beat her. If he was late and the food was cold, he would beat her. He told her to never leave him or he would hurt himself. My mom told me she stayed with him until his kids grew up and moved out of the house.

My mom met my dad not long after she left her husband and she got pregnant with me right away. She didn't think she could get pregnant because she had tried for sixteen years. She told me great things about my dad, but when I questioned her about him and why we didn't get to see him or why he wasn't around, she would show me her scars from where he beat her with a broken broomstick. My emotions annoyed her.

She taught me how to drive when I was ten. She said if she ever got too drunk I could take her car. The car was a stick shift, and when teaching me to drive she would tell my little sister she could hit me in the shoulder if I ground the gears. She showed me how to budget money, pay bills and hide money from her, because she would spend it all when she got drunk.

Even through her alcoholism, she tried to teach me things to make me self-reliant. She told me I would go to school and get a job. When I said I wanted to be a writer, she told me that writers don't make money and suggested I get a certificate as a flagger, because they made twenty-five dollars an hour. If I made my own money, I wouldn't have to rely on a man, and I could get a place and pay my own bills. She told me I should always make sure I could pay for everything so I didn't get stuck with a man if he ever hit me or left me.

Those were the most common evenings with my mom for the first ten years of my life. She later told me she only drank on weekdays so weekends could be family time. But for five days a week, I never knew what would happen.

My mom had parties, and sometimes she didn't come home and sometimes she dropped us off with random people who were our cousins or neighbours. She dropped us off with people who didn't take care of us properly or feed us. Sometimes they abused us or touched us in inappropriate ways.

I don't understand how my sister and I never ended up in foster care. It seemed like all of my friends did. It wasn't strange to hear someone say they were in foster care on our reserve, because most of the time they were still in the community, just with different caregivers.

We lived in a little house in town until I was six. When I think back to the things Evelyn and I did by ourselves, it is a miracle we didn't get picked up by someone. We wandered around our neighbourhood and down to the beach. We walked under the bridge by our little house and stopped to say hi to the people who lived there. Other times we walked up the hill to the corner store with the change we found to see what kind of candy we could buy.

There was a young couple, Randy and Edith, who lived close to the corner store we walked to. Sometimes we stopped at their house to visit. They introduced us to a record player and Michael Jackson and Cyndi Lauper. I had never seen a Black Forest ham in my life and thought they were fancy people. That little home was always quiet and calm. I'm sure they loved us and our visits. They were friends with my mom and our new stepdad, Joe Face.

My first dad in my memories wasn't my real dad, Kenzie, it was Joe Face, who was a good friend of Kenzie's. My real dad told me when I was older that Joe Face and my mom came to visit him in the hospital after a car accident, and my dad told them that they should get together. My mom hated it when my dad would share personal details with me.

My little sister and I loved our stepdad, and he was the first dad my sister knew. We loved his laugh and the way he took the time to play. He was an artist and used these big felt markers on different materials to draw eagles. He was one of Evelyn's inspirations to become an artist. He was a great man who filled a part of our lives I will never forget.

We travelled to Vancouver Island during the summer to visit his family. I loved the ferry rides with my little sister, but I feared the ocean and thought I would fall overboard if I ran outside. I was far too cautious, and understood danger and mortality even at six years old.

We picked berries and took speedboat rides to little islands around my stepdad's home community. We would lie on the beach after roasting hotdogs on an open fire and watch killer whales play in the ocean. I felt like a kid. I felt happy.

During one of those trips, we were driving at night in the city and my mom and our stepdad started to fight. They were yelling and hitting each other. They woke me up. Evelyn and I were sleeping in the back of our station wagon. I tried to keep her quiet. I peeked over the edge of the backseat to see if my mom was okay. My mom kicked him out of the car and drove off. She drove around for a while before she decided to go back and find him. We ran into a roadblock. There were emergency vehicles in the middle of the highway.

I looked over the edge of the backseat and watched a policeman approach our car. My mom asked him questions. She started to cry. I started to understand and pick things up from their conversation. A man had been drunk and staggering in the middle of the highway and got hit by a truck. I cried for my mom, but I don't remember what I said. My mom got mad at me and told me to lie back down. I knew it was bad.

I remember nothing else after that. I don't remember the funeral or where we went or what we did. I only remember that night when I lost another dad in my life, a man whose laugh I will never forget.

Soon we started spending more time at my tema's again. I loved my uncles and my tema. On top of listening to my tema's language and stories and teachings, I also learned how to box, run, fish, shoot arrows at targets, and play baseball and pool. I learned very early that I could not be weak, and tears were for sissies. I learned that pain was a long way from your heart, and it wasn't a good idea to cry for too long over anything.

My uncles did their best to toughen me up for school. They also told me to say bad words to my teachers and ask questions that would get me in trouble. I never did, because I was quiet—I was the kid who desperately needed acceptance. My first day at elementary school, I ran toward the door to my class. A little girl tripped me, her friends laughed at me, and she called me ugly. I fell flat on my face, embarrassed and hurt. I got a bleeding nose and knew I couldn't cry, so I got up and ran into the bathroom to clean myself up.

I hated that school.

It was a school where there were only a handful of Native kids, but I didn't grow up with them. They lived on other parts of the reserve so I'd never played with them.

I was five when people started to call me names. I didn't know what they meant. They used racial slurs that made no sense to me, but my heart broke every time. I always pretended I had a stomach ache to get out of class. I would sit on the concrete steps by the trash bin with my head between my legs, hyperventilating and dreading my classroom and the kids in it.

Girls pushed me into the coat rack—girls with perfect hair, cute noses and pretty clothes. They made fun of me every time I spoke because my stories didn't make sense to them and they asked me why I was so dirty all the time. The boys who were friends with them called me ugly and used phrases like "dirty Indian" and "wagon burner." I went home and asked my uncles what wagon burner meant, and they asked me who had called me that. My uncles were quick to give me a bunch of words to say back to them and told me that the next time they said anything like that, I should just punch them in the nose. They also told me that if I did punch them in the nose, I'd better be faster than they were.

My mom sent us to catechism, or Sunday school. We didn't have many Native kids there either, but I didn't get bullied and we got apple juice and cookies and listened to stories from the Bible. We liked our priests and nuns at St. Anne's, who gave us a little extra attention by giving us hot chocolate and letting us stay inside until our mom came to pick us up, because sometimes she was late or forgot about us.

My mom also sent me to gymnastics classes and baseball practice. Those were the worst because I didn't know anyone, and they were all white kids with blond hair and blue eyes and they weren't afraid to let me know that I didn't belong. I hated it when they walked by me and whispered things that made me sick to my stomach.

It was bad enough that I had to deal with white kids who didn't like me, but I had to deal with the Native kids from my reserve who were from the bigger families too. They all stuck together because they had the same last name. If I upset one of them, they all came after me. Sometimes they pretended to like me, and the next minute they would surround me and take turns hitting and kicking me and calling me names. It was a game to see who would be the first to make me cry. This made it a tough game for me to play, because my uncles also told me to never let them see me cry.

My uncles taught me how to fight the first time I came home with a black eye. They put boxing gloves on Evelyn and me to show us how to hold our fists and protect ourselves. They also told us how to throw a punch. My Uncle Louie loved to put boxing matches on the TV and tell us all about the greatest boxers of all time and what made them great. My uncle would say things in a way that made me feel like I could do anything or face anyone. There have been many times when I have summoned that power as I stood still, shaking with fear but knowing I had to get through it, even if it hurt.

When I think of the way kids treated me in my community, I also think of what my mom told me about understanding other people when they are mean and try to hurt me. She said that their anger and meanness was never about me.

I would think about my visits to some of these kids' homes and I knew that they went through the same things I did and even worse. When we were kids, they pretended to snort cocaine with cocoa powder. Some of them were only nine when they started to inhale gasoline fumes to get high. I saw naked people at parties in their home, women getting beat up by men, and kids getting thrown across the room and getting beat up by their own parents and relatives.

I was six when our community built a new subdivision called Westhills. It was during a time when our community settled a land claim and received a few million dollars. We didn't have a plan and right away many community members said they wanted payouts and per capita payments.

We were one of the few families who received a home. They were poorly built but brand new and big, and we were excited to live in a house that had stairs and a fireplace. My mom threw a big housewarming party and we had twenty people over to help break in the new home. Soon my mom had another boyfriend who was younger than her. He was short-tempered and cranky when he didn't have his drugs and alcohol. When they were sober we did some fun things together, but when they were drunk it was violent.

They both had moments when they would want to get sober. They took turns drinking and not drinking, but neither lasted long. One of the last fights they got into was when he came home drunk, yelling at my mom and threatening her, and she didn't back down. When he was drunk he terrified grown men as big as he was, but my mom refused to act scared.

I yelled at him from my bedroom, telling him to stop because he was scaring me. He yelled back at me to stop being a wimp. Pretty soon I heard crashing and struggling, and my mom was yelling at him and telling him she'd had enough of him. He hit her in the forehead and she hit him back and he fell to the ground. She picked up a side table and threw it on top of him before calling his brother who was across the street visiting their sister. His brother came over and she told him to take my mom's boyfriend out of her house before she called someone else.

As soon as they left, my mom came upstairs to the bathroom and I came out of my bedroom to see if she was okay. I screamed when I saw her because blood was dripping down her face and it seemed like she was bleeding really badly. She told me to stop crying and that it wasn't as bad as it looked. She grabbed a hand cloth to wipe her forehead. As she cleaned up her head, she looked at me and said, "You see! Never let a man hit you. If he does, you make sure you knock him down and kick him out."

I promised her that night no man would have any kind of power over me.

4

One of the most memorable turning points in my life happened just before I was ten. My mom decided to drop me off at teen social dance at the community hall before she went to the local bar. I had a sinking feeling I knew where she was going, so I reluctantly got out of the car and walked into the hall.

Almost immediately, I was surrounded by girls from the reserve, who pushed and kicked at me and wanted to know why I was there. I held myself together as they told me I was ugly and didn't belong there. At that time, I really felt like I didn't belong anywhere, and I did my best to shut down. I learned to stare blankly and go into my head to block out what was happening to me.

I was able to push past everyone and run outside. I hid underneath a staircase on the side of the community hall, and there I was able to let go and cry. I didn't cry too loud, because I didn't want anyone to find me.

While I was sitting in the dirt under the staircase, I tried to figure out what I was going to do. I didn't want to go back inside and I didn't want to wait under the staircase for hours. I was also afraid to walk in the dark to my tema's. It wasn't that far, but I knew there were dogs, bears, coyotes and cougars, and my uncles always told me that if I wandered in the dark, the trolls under the bridge would get me, or Owl Woman might come after me. I mapped out which way might be the safest and at what parts I'd have to run as fast as I could.

A car pulled up, its bright headlights shining directly on me. I tried to stay still and shrink into the shadows so they couldn't see me. It took me a moment to realize that someone was calling my name. It was my mom. Relieved, I climbed out from under the stairs and jumped into the passenger seat.

It had been a long time since I had felt safe with her, but at that moment I had so much gratitude for her coming back to check on me. She told me she was on her way to the bar but had a feeling that she had to come back, and decided to listen to her gut. She later said she felt proud of herself in that moment for putting her kid before her drinking.

Not long after, my mom told me she was going to treatment and would be gone for a while. She said she was going to get sober. I thought it was a nice idea, but I didn't put any hope into it. I was used to being let down and my mom rarely kept any of her promises. She told me I would stay with my tema and I had no problem with this.

My mom was gone for six to eight weeks, and she called us once a week to tell us some of the things she did. She said her room was small and she had to share it with someone else and it was a little uncomfortable for her. She also said that she spent a lot of time writing in a journal. I can't remember who drove us to see her in Prince George where she was finishing her program, probably because I had a hard time believing what I saw when we got there.

At the completion of my mom's treatment, I was confused because she looked so different. She was jumping and laughing openly. They were all asked to come to the front of the room to perform a silly skit for everyone. She played a saleswoman in a tampon commercial, and she couldn't stop laughing at the props they had made with a toilet paper roll, cotton and regular string.

My mom was happy. She looked fearless and she wasn't drunk. It is hard to remember my mom smiling and being affectionate when I was little. She was not an affectionate woman, but we knew she loved us.

Sometimes we would get cuddles and she would let us sleep with her, but she would also lose her temper really quickly and not want to be touched. Sometimes I would try to cuddle with her or sit next to her and she would push me away, telling me I was too close. She would say in an annoyed voice, "There's an entire room of places to sit. Why do you pick the spot right next to me?"

Seeing her with feelings and hearing her talk about them was confusing for me, and I wasn't sure if I could accept her new way of being. I didn't know what trust was, but I didn't trust her.

It was an interesting time getting to know my mom sober, because she started taking me to Alcoholics Anonymous meetings, the kinds of meetings where I listened to people talk about their lives and how hard they were. I listened to people talk about their drinking and how it was the root cause of all their suffering.

In my ten-year-old mind, it sounded fairly simple. Once they quit, their life was happy.

My mom asked me for forgiveness once and I gave it to her, even though I didn't really understand. I never understood anything, and my thinking had already been warped by my experiences.

My mom participated in a wide range of activities to keep her sober. She started going to AA roundups that gathered people together to share and celebrate and learn. She attended retreats and programs to help her work through some of the things she had experienced in her life.

At one point she decided to go to a gathering in the United States, and my godfather Adam Eneas and his wife Sandi Detjin took us with them to pick her up. The drive felt long. I was always intimidated by my godfather. He was a huge presence with a loud voice who naturally commanded attention.

My godfather is our hereditary chief and speaks the language fluently. My mom told me he was like a brother to her and her brothers because he was an only child. She was often jealous of the things he accomplished and would get upset when family tried to borrow money from him. I think it was more about her ego.

She had a hard time asking anyone for help. He was a successful businessman and was always dressed nice. He wore impressive jewellery, and everyone asked him for money.

He was also an elected chief and worked with the federal government. Before that, he was a part of the Red Power movement, which demanded self-determination for Indigenous peoples in the United States and Canada. He knew my dad and shared stories with me about meetings with government and other Indigenous leaders from across Canada.

He started the band office in Penticton with my mom after she went to night school to learn about office work.

One of the most inspiring speeches I ever heard from him was at the Okanagan Nation Alliance Annual General Assembly. There were approximately 300 people at the evening session honouring past and present leaders.

He walked up to the podium with Sandi and shared a little bit about his life and his experience in leadership as an alcoholic. He acknowledged and apologized for things he may have done in the past as a result of his alcoholism. It was the first time I witnessed a man of his stature and reputation share his vulnerability in a setting like that, in a room filled with people from his own community and nation.

Everyone in the room rose to their feet to give him a standing ovation, many with tears in their eyes. It is a moment I will always think back to.

I thought we were pretty special as little kids getting to ride in his car. We thought it was really fancy. We had ever been in a new car that had heat, air conditioning and a CD player.

Sandi was beautiful; her face was bright and full of smiles and love. Every chance she got, she gave hugs to the people around her and made sure to squeeze them tight. I have never met another woman like her in my life. She shared her music with us and kept turning around to make sure we were okay. I didn't know it was possible for one person to have so much love to share with everyone. She became a role model to me for so many reasons, including her example and dedication to her sobriety and service work that has helped save so many lives.

I should have been happy with the changes happening in my life. But of course, a child of an alcoholic doesn't just go back to being a kid overnight. I had spent my entire life taking care of things, taking care of myself and my little sister, and all of a sudden I had this mom who was present and wanted to do things for me and give me rules.

She wanted to set boundaries and curfews. She no longer got dropped off downtown, giving me a fifty- or hundred-dollar bill to keep me occupied while she went to the bar or bingo, and I didn't have to steal money from her to hide anymore. All the things I learned to survive were no longer needed, but I still didn't feel confident that things had changed for good.

My mom was still with her boyfriend, and he managed to stay sober for a year and a half with her. Of all our stepdads, he was the one I connected with. He was a deep thinker and read a lot of books and talked to me about science. He had magazines about astrology that I would read, and a telescope that he would let us use.

Having him sober was comforting, but there were times when he would get really cranky. My mom would get fed up and load us into the car to bring him to his friend who gave him money because he had a lease with him, then my mom would drive him downtown to the arcade to get his weed. It was that experience that made me hate weed, because it made people cranky and mean.

My stepdad had a daughter who we immediately took as our baby sister. We wanted to keep her forever; we thought she was the cutest live doll, always full of energy and tons of questions. I didn't know any little girl who talked as much as she did. Even at that age I thought she was a genius.

He was still around when I started to talk back to my mom and run away. I started smoking when I was ten. I would sneak cigarettes from her and eventually just buy my own. Back then you could walk into the store as a kid, say you were buying cigarettes for your parents and they would sell you a pack for $2.50.

My stepdad was there to witness me drinking alcohol for the first time. I was twelve. It was over the summer, and my older sister Teri had come to visit. My real dad was living in Penticton in a hotel at the time and I desperately wanted to connect with my sister and be accepted by her.

My best friend Karen and I gave her some money to buy beer and we went to a playground by the beach to drink. Before I knew it, there were others there who had brought hard alcohol and were offering it to us. I decided to try it all.

I was brought home kicking and screaming by one of our community members, who knew it wasn't right to see a twelve-year-old completely wasted. She threw me in the back of her car, and I kicked and screamed when she pulled up to my house, got out and rang the doorbell. I tried to get out of the car and run away, but I was so drunk I couldn't control my body and stayed in the car.

I saw my stepdad come to the door and look out into the car. All I saw was him strolling to the car quickly and opening the door to grab me. He carried me into the house, plopped me down on my bed and left. A minute later my mom came into my room, yelling at me and wanting to know how much I'd had to drink.

The next day my mom brought me to my dad's place to tell him about my night. She spent the next few days talking to me about alcoholism and brought me to an Alcoholics Anonymous meeting with her. I had feelings of shame for the way I acted, and I laughed at myself with my friends about how crazy things got. It didn't stop me from wanting to drink, and from that day forward I found myself trying to find people to drink with who would accept me into their circles.

By the time school started again, I was done. I hated school and I always skipped classes and yelled at my teachers. I was so angry for so many reasons. I hated the way the other kids made me feel and I hated the way the teachers talked to me and made me feel stupid and worthless.

I always wanted to be a good student. I always strived to get good grades. I remember trying so hard to study, but I had so many distractions in my life that I could never really focus. When it came to math, I just didn't understand it.

My teachers continually told me I was a problem. Whenever a white kid would say something to me, I would react. Sometimes I would threaten them and other times I would just walk right up to them and punch them in the face, sending me to the principal's office.

I was also that kid who sat on the top of my chair and questioned what they taught in social studies about Indigenous peoples. I constantly told the teachers they were teaching crap and I was routinely sent out of the room because I was a troublemaker.

On more than one occasion, a teacher told me I was never going to amount to anything, and sometimes I believed them. There were other times that I knew deep down inside they had no idea who I was.

I continued to run away and drink. I would kiss any boy who called me beautiful and quickly became known as easy. I didn't understand why they didn't ask me out or want to date me or call me their girlfriend. Every time I hooked up with someone, they pretended not to know me afterward.

At age twelve, it became an addiction for me to find love. I hitchhiked from town to town, from Penticton to Chase to Kamloops to Prince George, following groups of people who paid attention to me and allowed me into their circles.

I partied with people who were near the legal drinking age, many of them eighteen to twenty-one years old. I was barely thirteen. My dad ended up leaving Penticton and moving to Kamloops. My older sister moved with him and took on the role of his caretaker and nurse. When I asked to live with him, I had to take on some of the responsibilities of caring for my father, who was a quadriplegic.

My dad was in a car accident when I was two or three years old. No one ever gave me details of the accident, but I believe he was drinking and driving and had run off the road, ending upside down on the side of a hill until the paramedics found him. My dad told my sister Teri that he remembered struggling and moving around until they moved him to get him out of the car.

He moved from hospitals to senior-living complexes to one-bedroom apartments where homecare nurses would come check on him, and his nephews would stay to take care of him. Sometimes they would find a big van, take out the back seats, put a mattress in it and load my dad inside to take him visiting people all over British Columbia.

One of my favourite memories was when I was seven years old at Okanagan beach in Penticton with Evelyn. A young man I recognized came up to me and told me he was my cousin and that my dad was with him. We followed him to the van. The back doors were open, and there was my dad. He told me and Evelyn to get in so he could take us to Burger King for mini burgers. We only saw my dad once a year, and usually it was when my mom would take us to visit him in a hospital.

My dad still drank, and there were times Teri would drink with him and I would sneak alcohol. When my dad passed out, we would head out to find our friends or they would come visit us at our apartment.

My sister dated a guy who hung out with a tight-knit group of boys. They sang at powwows and travelled anywhere their old cars would take them. Everyone loved them. On the weekdays and weekends they weren't at a powwow, they would party.

They had a reputation for hooking up with various girls and then joking with one another about it, because they would take turns hooking up with the same girl. I was starved for love and ended up being one of those girls.

I don't know who I lost my virginity to, because the room was dark and I couldn't see. There was a group of eight to ten of us sleeping in one giant room and I was put in a position where I couldn't make a sound. I didn't want to be shunned by the group, so I stayed quiet and didn't say anything. That moment was one of the biggest shames I have carried through my life.

When I was taking care of my dad, he would share stories with me about his days with the Red Power movement. He talked about sellouts and government. He told me stories about Indigenous-rights activists Russell Means and Leonard Peltier. I don't remember the details, but I knew he was always worried about being listened to. Every few days he would make me do weird things like dial random numbers into the phone and listen for clicking. If there was a click, he would get me to dial some more numbers and hang up, and then dial the number he wanted. He told me it was to make sure the phone wasn't tapped by federal-government agents.

One evening I had a really bad headache and asked my dad if he had any Tylenol. He told me to find the bottle of blue pills in his closet. He told me to take half a pill and drink some water, which I did. In about ten minutes I felt numb and disconnected. I found out it was valium, and I was hooked from the moment I swallowed it. I would steal his pills, and there were times I would go to the pharmacy to get refills for him and tell them he needed extra pills because he would always run out. It didn't take long before the pharmacist called my dad and he called the cops on me.

I ended up moving to Chase with my sister, her boyfriend and his mom. His mom was the only person who had a steady job in the house, and people showed up to crash there and eat the food. My sister would buy food to hide under her bed and in her closet, because there were many times when there was no food in the house.

During those times, I would walk half an hour into the village and use a payphone to call my mom collect and ask her for money or to pick me up. Sometimes she would send me an envelope through the Greyhound bus so I could buy a bus ticket home, and I'd use the extra money to go eat fries and gravy. Sometimes she would drive the three hours to pick me up and bring me home, and other times she would yell at me for being stupid and called me names to shame me, hoping it would make me come home.

The things she would say to me made me feel humiliated and hurt and unloved, so I would hang up and continue with what I was doing. I would go for a week, drinking when I could and popping pills, telling myself over and over that no one loved me, not even my mom. I used the things she said to put myself in harm's way because I didn't think anyone cared about me.

Eventually I ended up back home again. My mom would always take me for a cruise to talk to me about what I was going through. She would share what she learned about being an alcoholic.

She would tell me that I couldn't keep things inside and that I needed to let them out. She said that keeping them inside and stuffing them down was like a bottle filled with pop. If you keep filling it and filling it, eventually it's going to explode, and the only person who is going to get hurt is yourself.

She promised me I would feel better if I just let everything out. Every time she said those things I would get frustrated, because I didn't think there was anything I needed to let out. I didn't feel I was holding anything in my mind; I was just trying to have fun.

It was around that time that I lost my tema. She passed away at home in her bed, and I got the phone call in the afternoon. I think it was the last time I really cried. I knew my tema was in her eighties, but I had expected her to live another twenty years.

When I look back to all the safe and happy times I ever had, they always involved my tema. I remember the way she would talk to me and laugh and joke, the way she would rub my back and tell me stories. She could be serious, but it didn't last long because she always had something silly to say. I still miss the sound of her Indian songs and prayers.

I did my best to stay sober after she passed away. I felt so much shame for the things I did and said when I was drinking. I never thought of the hurt I put my mom through. Even though she did her best to convey her feelings to me, I had a hard time feeling bad for her.

It must have driven her mad to work so hard to break the cycle of addiction and disease, only to have her daughter continue on her own crazy path.

My mom decided the only way she could connect with me and help keep me sober was by taking me to powwows. We were used to attending the small traditional powwows in B.C., and my mom wanted to show us what it was like to really powwow.

She put time into outfits for me and my sister and she applied for cultural support to bring us to powwows across Canada and the United States. When that help was no longer available, she took payroll advances and borrowed money. My mom had complete faith in our culture and language, and she knew that travelling and meeting other people would connect us to who we were and ground us there.

My mom had helped organize some of the first powwows in B.C. She became close with Steven and Gwen Point from the Sto:lo Nation, and they supported each other when it came to organizing their powwows. She also travelled to Germany with Ernie Phillips to dance. Ernie was a well-known powwow dancer who travelled across the country. He taught many people how to make outfits and dance. He is still alive today and lives in Chase, British Columbia. My mom was connected with people all over the place. Whenever I told my mom I had met someone new, she would ask who their parents were. In most cases my mom knew them.

When I was fourteen, I decided to run for powwow princess. I often compare the experience to rodeo royalty or city princess pageants. I've never been in either, but I assume they're similar—there are commitments and rules you have to follow, and you have to speak publicly, fundraise and have a talent of some sort.

During my contest, I spoke my language and read my poetry and the judges picked me. I knew that I had a lot of responsibilities and was going to be held to a higher standard, because now I was considered a role model and ambassador for that powwow and its committee. My mom told me I had to hold my crown with dignity and that I didn't just represent myself, I represented my family, community and nation.

I promised not to drink or take part in any other type of questionable behaviour. My mom had worked hard to get me focused on something other than boys and partying.

She had found something to keep me centred and sober. I was proud of myself. I couldn't wait to travel, meet people and hear the singers and the beat of the drums. I loved the smell of the buckskin and the earth getting kicked up. My mom would tell us that our job was to stay in the dance arena, pay attention and watch the dancers, and always find a place to sit beside elders.

We would leave for a powwow right after my mom finished work, and every once in a while she would take Friday off so we could leave earlier. Powwows always started by seven p.m. on Fridays. If we were lucky the powwow would end as early as eleven p.m. on Sunday, but sometimes, if it was a big powwow, it didn't end until three a.m.

Powwows have dance categories. In the women's categories there are three styles. Traditional dance is slow moving, and the dancers wear buckskin and lots of beadwork. Jingle-dress dance is a little quicker; the feet stay close to the ground and the dancers wear dresses with cones sewn on to make the sound of rain. Fancy-shawl dancers are fast and extremely athletic; the dancers wear shawls and are often referred to as butterfly dancers.

We didn't always stay until the end, because we were just beginning to fancy-shawl dance and it was a style that was highly competitive. Evelyn and I never really took to it and we didn't place in competition. It wasn't until Evelyn started to dance in the traditional category that we had to stay and wait for winners to get announced, because she always placed in her category.

Powwows gave me something to look forward to and to be proud of, because at home I still struggled with school during the weekdays and was still dealing with racism. Being involved in powwow helped me deal with the bigotry, because I knew that the people and culture I come from is beautiful and unique.

We would get to the powwow just before the time for Grand Entry. Sometimes we didn't get there until after the first day of the powwow was over, because the drive had taken so long and we would have to set up our tent in the powwow campground in the dark. We travelled with a giant ugly green army tent that kept cool in the summer. My mom had labelled all the poles so we could set it up quickly. It never took us long, because we all knew our jobs.

My mom was always prepared, and she would stay at our camp and cook for us. I always felt spoiled because she would always have hot food for us at the camp. When she wasn't with us, we lived off of bologna sandwiches and chips.

My mom made sure we always made Grand Entry on time. Everyone had to be fully dressed in their outfits and beadwork, feathers and braids. My mom told me that we had to stay in the circle the whole time. Many dancers back then were very disciplined. It was respectful to stay in the circle until all the opening business was taken care of, including the prayer and invocation. Sometimes there was a lot of official talking and people would get annoyed and sit down, but my mom was really strict when it came to listening.

Sometimes it was an elder who shared their teachings or prophecies, and sometimes it was an elected leader from the community who talked about politics and the current state of our people. Sometimes it was a medicine person who explained protocols and proper ways of doing things that young people were not doing anymore. One of the teachings we had was to stay clean and sober if you wanted to dance. Elders always reminded us of the importance of sobriety when it came to our culture. There were times when an elder would hear of a young dancer or drum group partying during the powwow, and they would approach them and take their drum or their feathers and beadwork away until they learned to respect the powwow circle. It was far stricter when I was younger, and I don't think these things happen anymore.

My mom became the world to me. She was always there for me when I needed a shoulder to cry on, and she always had the perfect words for me. Her wisdom—in person or shared in letters—and her calmness always made me believe that everything was going to be okay.

My mom's home became a safe place for everyone. People would visit her and ask for her advice or to run things by her, including the members of our leadership. Our friends always knew our door was open, and when things weren't great at home they knew she would let them stay with us.

Dancers and singers and ceremony people who were driving through Penticton knew they could always stop at our house, and she would make sure they had a place to sleep, eat and shower. She had a presence about her that provided comfort, because when she said something it would happen. She always found a way to get things done. She would tell me, "Don't stop just because someone tells you no. You always find a way to go around, under, over and through."

The quality I remember most about my mom was her ability to communicate to us through her lectures. It's an aspect of her that most of my friends remember too. Any time she told us to get in the car and go for a cruise, we knew she was going to lecture us about something. Many times, I scanned my brain to see if I had done something wrong so I could think of a way to defend myself.

Most of the time she just wanted to share what she had been thinking or what she had learned that week. She always told us it was good to learn from different people. She would tell us that sometimes you learn the most profound things from people you don't even like. Usually when we don't like someone, we shut our mind off to everything they say or find ways to make them wrong and not agree with them.

She never wanted us to stay on the reserve. She said it was like living in a fishbowl—everyone watched what you did. She said if we stayed on the reserve all the time we wouldn't experience new things, and we would get tunnel vision. When we stay in one place it's hard to grow. Everyone starts thinking the same way and we get mob mentality.

She loved our community and nation, and she was friends with everyone. She said that there was a lot of hurt our people had to get through and we needed to have understanding. She would tell me some of the stories she heard from friends and family about their experiences growing up, and she understood why certain people acted in certain ways. There were people who gossiped and said mean things, but she always told us there was a reason and not to take it personally.

My mom wanted us to go to school and travel the world before we settled down. She always did her best to take us places, even if she didn't always have enough money.

She told us we had to work hard and that sometimes that meant being open to learning from everyone, even if we didn't agree with them, because it is always good to know a little something about everything.

Our mom told us that she did not want us to ever go on welfare because it didn't pay enough, and once you go on it you get stuck. She explained that was the way it was set up: to keep us dependant and in poverty.

She said we had enough skills to always be able to do something to get by. She said that if we had to, we could pick cherries in the summertime and bead in the wintertime. I hated picking cherries in the summer, because she would wake us up before the sun came up and take us to an orchard to pick cherries until noon before it got too hot. We learned how to set up ladders and concentrate on picking the cherries with the stems, and then bring the pails in to get weighed. In 1987, each pail of cherries got us two dollars. We usually made about twenty to thirty dollars per day.

She would take us home to grab our bathing suits and drop us off at the beach. She always gave us the money we made to spend at the food concession.

We spent the next couple of years getting close and building trust. There were many times we didn't get along, but my mom became skilled at working through conflict with me.

We continued to travel to powwows together, and when I got my driver's licence she would tell me and my sister to take our white minivan and go to the powwow without her. We would bring our friends with us and travel during the summer, continuing to stay out of trouble.

5

Growing up, my tema, my uncles and my mom always said, "Don't be full of yourself and do not be vain." I think it's why I was told I was funny-looking. I was rarely ever told I was beautiful as a child. Growing up on the reserve, I was told daily that I was ugly, dirty and funny-looking, and it continued into my early school days.

Being told the same thing over and over again, I started to believe it. I grew up hating everything about myself. After school, I would get home and take a bath three times. I would fill the tub and scrub my skin, and then empty it when it got too cold and add more hot water and scrub my skin some more, hoping it would get lighter.

I craved love and someone wanting me. I just wanted to be taken care of, because I was tired of doing all the caretaking. I craved love, even though I didn't know what it felt like. I was raised not to feel things, because when you don't feel, you won't get hurt, cry or care.

When I was fourteen I started to date Davis, one of the guys I hung out with on our reserve. We were together for four years. He thought I was sixteen because I drove my mom's car everywhere. She didn't know I would take the car off the reserve and drive into town to pick up my friends.

Davis became my best friend. We had always known each other, as we grew up together, but we had never hung out until I came back from spending time with my older sister and my dad.

Davis's mom and my tema went to church together, and the kids would all play outside in the park before and after Sunday Mass. One thing I remembered most about Davis was how mean he was at that time, and that continued right into high school. He liked to tease people until they got really upset or came close to crying before he would stop.

When I began spending time with him and our larger group of friends, we would hang out and do nothing. Sometimes we would watch movies, go for drives, sit out under the stars, or go skiing during the winter. He taught me how to ride dirt bikes and how to drive fast. We played video games and floor hockey, basketball and pool. We did everything together.

The group of guys we hung out with were all from the same family, one of the smaller ones in our community. We would all meet up at their cousin's place in town and we would figure out what to do there. We would head to the beach and hang out or go wander downtown.

Other times the guys would decide to do break-and-enters. It took me a while to figure out what they were talking about, and even longer to figure out what "B&E" meant. Occasionally, a few other girls and I were allowed to go with them, but we had to stay in the car and keep an eye out.

We had a friend with a cousin who would get out of jail for a week or two once in a while. He had been in jail since we were kids. He was a big guy with tattoos who intimidated anyone who came across him. But whenever my mom would see him, she would smile and call him Shorty.

He knew how to steal cars and would find one to take us joyriding in, or he would go with the other boys to steal dirt bikes and golf carts. They made the newspapers all the time and pretty soon everyone's parents were telling their kids not to hang out with us.

Other days we would stay in and watch movies. Some films we could watch over and over again, like *Young Guns.* Or we would sit in the kitchen and play Crazy Eights.

Every once in a while, the mom of the house would be home from her travels and we would behave ourselves. Everyone called her Lee, or Mom. We never grew up calling adults Mr. or Mrs. So-and-So, but it was never considered disrespectful.

Lee rarely came out of her room unless it was to get a coffee and something to eat. I asked her son what she was doing and he told me she was writing a book. I immediately became starstruck, even though I didn't know her outside of being the mom who took us all in. I hadn't even read a book of hers yet. I wanted to know everything about her and how she had become a writer. Sometimes she would sit for a moment and say hi. Their family was always making jokes and loved to laugh.

She was really good at not letting us distract her for too long. I think she was writing her novel *Ravensong,* a story of a young woman caught between her people's traditional ways and white society's values during a deadly flu epidemic in the '50s. She became one of my biggest writing inspirations. I wouldn't know until later in my life exactly who she was and how she influenced writers all across our country.

I found out later on that she knew my dad, Kenzie. Her brother-in-law was my stepdad, Joe Face, and she had stories about the '70s that she captured in her book *I Am Woman.* This book strongly influenced a man who would become my second husband.

Eventually, I grew restless and didn't want to stick around our town anymore. My mom called it itchy feet, and said it was one of the things she really didn't like about me, because it reminded her of my dad. She thought I was running away from something, and she told me that when I came back it would still be there. I thought she didn't know what she was talking about.

She told me my dad could never stay in one place. My desire to travel and move was the one thing that got in the way of most of my relationships. I didn't understand my mom's dislike for the times I took off, especially when she had told me she didn't want me to become stuck on the reserve.

Davis hated it when I left to powwow, because he didn't understand powwow culture or know anything about it. He grew up strictly Catholic and didn't like to travel. We went back and forth about that, but I hoped he would enjoy travelling one day, and he hoped that I would settle down and stay in one place.

At the end of the summer of 1994, I began feeling tired and sick. I couldn't figure out what was wrong with me, so I went to my doctor. He took a few tests and I went home. He told me it might just be a flu, but he would call me if anything came up.

A few days later, the doctor called and told me he wanted me to come in. He sat me down and told me I was pregnant. I didn't even realize I had taken a pregnancy test; the thought hadn't even crossed my mind. I walked out of the doctor's office and right past Davis, who had given me a ride.

He had no idea what was happening. He quickly followed me and asked if I was okay. I was speed-walking down the staircase and told him, "I'm pregnant." He went quiet and let out a little profanity.

We jumped into his car and sat there, quiet, looking at the mountain in the background. I grabbed a cigarette and lit it up, and he immediately tried to grab it and throw it away. I stopped him with a deadly look and told him, "Just let me have this last one."

He retreated and sank back into his seat. He offered to take me into the mountains and hide there. He told me he could hunt and that we would be okay. I burst out laughing and realized we had to tell my mom right away while she was at work, so she couldn't hurt us.

We took a long ten-minute drive from the doctor's office to the band office. When we got there, I told Davis to sit in the coffee room and wait for me to call him in.

After pausing and trying to find ways to get my mom to guess what my news was, I told her what happened and she instructed me to bring Davis in. She looked him dead in the eyes and called him "Dad." His knees buckled and he went pale, and my mom laughed at his reaction.

It took me a long time to process my feelings. There were so many reasons why I felt ashamed of getting pregnant at seventeen. I thought of all the messaging around teen pregnancy. I didn't believe I had a choice at the time and the only option was to have the baby, so I didn't wonder if I would stay pregnant, I wondered what I was going to do.

I was holding a princess crown for a powwow an hour away from where we lived. I felt bad because of the high expectations put on powwow royalty. We were even told we weren't allowed to have a boyfriend, and I remember people telling stories of girls who got pregnant while carrying a crown and being shamed for it.

I was really lucky. I brought my crown to the powwow committee and told them I needed to give it back because I was expecting. They smiled, congratulated me, and told me to keep it until the time came to give it up at the powwow.

Once I faced my fear and dealt with the committee and my crown, I felt a sense of relief and was able to enjoy my pregnancy.

For most of my life my mom always told me to never get pregnant like those other poor girls. She always told me she would never take care of any grandkids. It was obvious she had no idea how excited she would be. She took care of me, continued to support me, and encouraged me to take care of myself. She was also really honest with me about her expectations that I was not to go on welfare or expect her to take care of me financially.

She wanted me to take distance learning and get as much of my Grade 10 and 11 done as possible before the baby came. She also wanted me to get a job, and I ended up getting a part-time position at the band office as an education assistant. I would work in the mornings, do schoolwork in the afternoon, and mail off my work once a week.

In June 1995, at the age of eighteen, I gave birth to Kyle. His dad was there, along with his two grandmothers. They were the first to hold him and welcome him into the world in our language. They told him how loved he was, how special he was, and how we were waiting for him to come here. They did this so that no matter what happened, he would always have those words as the first things he heard. He would always know who he was and where he came from and where he belonged. My mom took his belly button after it fell out and took care of it for us to connect him to the land.

Later on, when I would ask Kyle if my drinking and leaving ever made him feel unwanted, he told me he spent his life always feeling like he was wanted. I know it's because of the love he received from his grandmothers on the day he was born.

6

I didn't stay with Davis for long. I ended up quickly moving on and dating other people shortly after Kyle's birth. As the years have gone by, I've learned that in order to feel loved, you have to feel it for yourself first. At eighteen, I expected others to make me feel loved and wanted, and if they didn't I would find someone who would.

Davis was a hard worker. From the moment I met him he let me know his work was the most important thing to him, and his days were fourteen to sixteen hours. My mom used to tell me his parents must have squished bees and rubbed them all over him when he was a baby to make him a hard worker.

When I had our son, Davis bought us a little old blue four-door car that required a lot of work, and the first chance I had I took it to a powwow in Washington. It ended up breaking down, and when I called home to let Davis know, he told me to come home right away.

When I told him that I would be home after the powwow was over, he told me I had to come home or he was going to break up with me.

The moment I heard that, my heart went numb. I felt like he betrayed me by giving me an ultimatum, hoping I would stay because we had a baby. I shut down and acted like I didn't care. It was always my first response when my heart broke. It always felt like blood leaving my body, and then a wall of nothingness would come up around me.

I knew that I did care and that I hurt, but I was taught to hide all of those feelings, so I hung up the phone and that was it. I was not allowed to let a man tell me what to do.

It wasn't long before I began looking for someone else to love me. I started to talk to people I met on the internet through a web forum called Native American Chat.

I met a guy named Billy who lived in Arizona. Eventually he asked me to come meet him and offered to buy my plane ticket. Looking back on my life, I realize how many times I put myself in a position to be greatly harmed. There were times when I was hurt and assaulted, but I lived and often blamed myself. Many times, I was too embarrassed about what had happened and kept it a secret.

I was lucky this time. I was nineteen and he was only two years older and going to university. He was close with his family, had a great sense of humour, and was generally just a nice guy. We had a great time and laughed together. We started making trips to see each other. I never did tell him I had a son, because he had made a comment during one of our first conversations about kids and his desire to not have any.

He was funny and always told me how pretty I was, and that was all I needed at the time to make me feel worthy and wanted. As I got to know him, I thought that he was much too nice for me. Coming from a great family, I thought there was no way he was going to want to stay in a relationship with me, because I was a little messed up and struggling with my guilt about being unsure how to be a mom.

I decided the relationship wouldn't last, but that I would make the most of it while I could. It did not take much for me to completely throw myself into a relationship. I was really good at being something others wanted me to be, but only for a short time.

I planned a trip to Arizona on Christmas and was leaving really late at night. I had to drive from my home in Penticton to Seattle, which was a nine-hour drive in the winter.

My mom had been sick for the previous three months. She took a month off of work and couldn't even get out of bed to make turkey. The only thing she was able to eat was soup. It was the first year I did the whole turkey dinner by myself.

She had been in and out of the hospital around that time. Once she fainted and the ambulance came to get her. She was having weird spells and the doctors kept telling her it was the flu.

On Christmas night, when I was leaving, I went into my mom's room and told her I was getting on the road and asked her for some gas money. She told me to grab her wallet and take some cash.

She sat up to give me a hug and looked at me, really confused. She told me she wasn't drunk. I thought it was her medication making her loopy and I told her I knew she wasn't drunk, that she just needed to get some sleep because it was late.

Ten hours later, while I was at the Seattle airport, my old Nokia cellphone rang and my little sister told me that Mom had a stroke. I didn't know what to say because I had no idea what a stroke was, and my mind was darting all over the place trying to figure it out. I asked if she was okay.

The line went quiet. Someone else grabbed the phone and said, "Elaine, you need to come home. Your mom had a stroke. She is brain dead. You have to come home right now."

I started writing this book when I was thirty. It took me two years to write that experience with my mom and it still affects my whole being.

For fourteen years, I blamed myself for what happened to my mom. I thought I should have known better. I couldn't believe I was so stupid. How could I not know? After her stroke I spent ten years torturing myself for what happened to my mom.

As I drove home, I couldn't stop thinking about my mom being brain dead. I had no idea what a stroke was at the time. I thought it might be something terrible that happened to people, but something they could recover from. I was sure that I had heard people in my community mention someone who'd had a stroke who was still functioning and living in the community. I didn't think it was that serious. I didn't have WebMD at the time to research it, and I could feel myself shutting down.

When I got back to Canada, a big storm had already started. I made it to Abbotsford before the roads were completely shut down.

I managed to find a place to get off the highway and found myself at a Best Western. I pulled into the parking lot and listened to the radio announce that all major highways were closed, along with bus depots and airports.

I phoned home and got hold of our band manager, who was also a friend of my mom's, and told him what was happening. He had already heard what happened. He also knew that she had been sick.

He told me to let him talk to the front desk. Hotels everywhere were sold out, but while we were on the phone there was a cancellation. He managed to get me a room and allowed me to charge my stay and dinner to his credit card, because all I had was the gas money my mom had given me to get to Seattle.

I was stuck in the hotel for four days watching the road report and not wanting to call home, waiting for the red lines on the map to turn orange so I could get back on the road.

As soon as the roads opened, I went out to my car. It was covered in a foot of snow with a layer of ice on top. It took me a long time to chip the ice off and get the snow off my car. I had very little experience driving in the snow; I did not think of the road conditions or what they would be like after being closed for four days.

I didn't even know that my all-season tires weren't suitable for driving on the connector between the Lower Mainland and the Interior, which was called the "highway of hell" for a reason. It remains the most horrific experience I have ever had on any highway, and I have had many since then.

After a twelve-hour drive that usually takes only two and a half hours, I finally made it back to Penticton. My mom was still in the hospital and I learned that she had two massive aneurysms in her brain that caused her to have a major stroke. She would never be able to talk to me again.

Evelyn was devastated, because when they got to the hospital, the attendant said if she had come in sooner they might have been able to give her something to prevent the damage from being so severe. Hearing those words traumatized my sister and me for the majority of our young adulthood.

I went home and fell asleep. When I woke up late in the afternoon the next day, I staggered out past our backyard and walked until I found a tree away from our house and the houses around us.

I cried so hard I couldn't breathe. I sat there and cried and yowled with anger and sadness. I couldn't stop wondering why God would do this to my mom. I didn't understand how this could happen when we had such a strong faith in God and the Creator.

I prayed and prayed and then gave up. I gave up hope, and without knowing it I gave up faith. That night, I went to the bar and got drunk.

For the next two years I drank myself into oblivion. I drank to black out. I got into fistfights and spent all of my money. I didn't care if I had bills to take over or groceries to buy. I gave up on myself and began to see Kyle less and less, as he was staying with his grandparents.

I blamed myself so much; I called myself selfish. I was a victim again. I had grown up taking care of myself and my sister, and now, at the age of nineteen, I was left to do it again. I was full of resentment and anger. I felt sorry for myself and blamed everyone in my life for where I was at.

I had no idea how to deal with my mom's affairs. I didn't even think about it. I had my mom's bank card and I knew her code, so I just continued to use it to buy groceries and party.

Eventually her friends would ask me about something as if I should have known that I should be taking care of it, but I had no clue. It didn't even cross my mind to worry about her car and insurance payments and whatever debt she was holding.

I made all my decisions right in my mind by telling myself that my mom would want us to be taken care of.

She stayed in the hospital for a few months, had a few surgeries, and started physical therapy. Then a meeting was called with me and my mom's stepchildren to talk about her arrangements.

When she came home to live with us, they sent nurses and therapists over to show us how to take care of her. I was nineteen and my sister was seventeen.

In the beginning, we fell into the routine of taking care of her. My mom had a hard time letting us do things for her, like helping her with the bathroom and bathing. Evelyn was really good at doing stretches with her to keep her joints limber.

There were so many times when I would break and take off to drink. My mom knew what I was doing, and my sister continually prayed for me. I had no control over myself or my life. The things that I used to care about didn't mean anything, and the people I used to worry about disappointing also meant nothing. Every time someone tried to intervene and talk to me, I sat quietly, stewing in anger, wondering what the hell they expected from me. Who did they think they were? No one was ever there to help us when we needed it.

One of my mom's best friends called me and told me to come to the band office to meet with her. She shut the door, sat down, and asked me how I was doing. I let her know I was okay.

She asked me if I had any plans besides taking care of my mom and I said no. I didn't dare think beyond that, because to me, not taking care of her meant that she was no longer with us.

Her friend looked at me and told me my mom loved my sister and me more than anything in the world, and the one thing she wanted for us was to get an education and become something. She said she knew that my mom didn't want us to get stuck there. I hated school but I decided to look into it because it was what my mom wanted. I decided to go back to school and people assured me that my mom would be taken care of. I didn't realize that I was leaving Evelyn again, not knowing she would end up being the one to take care of our mom while I was gone.

I had a few schools in mind, but going to school in Canada meant completing a bunch of upgrading and I found out that I could get into a post-secondary institution in the States by taking an exam for mature students. It wasn't long after I returned home that I stopped talking to Billy. I didn't have much hope for the relationship, because I was so messed up and now I had more responsibility at home. Billy was extremely carefree, and I didn't want to burden him. Shortly after I stopped talking to him, I started talking to a man in Idaho who was ten years older than me. We had met a few times, so I decided to go to school in Pocatello, Idaho.

We lived a dysfunctional, addicted lifestyle together and acted like no one knew. For many reasons, my family and friends back home questioned what I was doing with him. I challenged them by asking what they were trying to say.

We were introduced to each other because he was a powwow singer and dancer. He was a really good dancer and usually placed in the competitions or was otherwise recognized or honoured. He also sang with one of the drum groups that I had idolized growing up. People always held him and his family in high regard, and their family name was well known.

We went to powwows on the weekend and drank on the weekdays. There were days that I didn't see him because he would drink and not come back. He ended up in jail for a month when I first moved in with him because of traffic tickets for driving under the influence. When he got out of jail, I had to drive him to the casino where he worked as a security guard.

When he drank, he became one of those sloppy drunks that I saw when I was a kid. Many times he was so drunk he didn't even know who I was. He couldn't focus or talk, and he would black out and often pee the bed. I would wake up, shower, change my clothes and sleep on the floor. I told myself I would never be that bad. His grandma told me that if I knew how to be a good woman, he wouldn't be doing those things. His mother and grandmother didn't think much of me, and they didn't think I was good enough for him.

I got pregnant in that relationship. I couldn't think of anything more horrible than being stuck with that man for the rest of my life. I was also angry because he told me he was unable to have children because of an accident at work.

I was angry because deep down I knew I didn't belong there. I ended up making a decision that would add to the regret and shame that had become my life. I told him I had to go back to Canada right away and see a doctor while I was there. When I arrived, I made an appointment to have an abortion. Until that day I didn't believe in getting an abortion, and had truly believed in the sacredness in life, that the Creator didn't give you more than you could handle. However, by that point in my life I didn't believe any of that was true.

Even after the abortion, I went back to Idaho. I told him that I was going to get my own place off the reserve so that I was closer to school. It wasn't until our relationship got abusive and he started pushing me and throwing me around that I decided I was going to leave.

I went home for the holidays, but he wasn't allowed to come with me because his DUIs prevented him from crossing the border. The first night I got back to Penticton, I went straight to the bar and met a young man that everyone called Kasp, but I refused to do so and called him by his name, Rob. He went back to the States with me to pack up the rest of my things.

I didn't know much about Rob. I knew he had lived a hard life and was coping with loss and childhood trauma. His story was unbelievable, but at the time I didn't care because he was good company at the club when we first met. I didn't want anyone tying me down because I had just gotten out of a bad relationship that lasted longer than it should have.

We stayed together for fourteen years. We both drank and abused each other, cheated on each other, manipulated and lied to each other and clung on to each other because we didn't want to be alone.

I tried many times in my twenties to get sober. I would think of my mom and I would do my best to quit on my own. Each time I tried, I would make it to the one-year mark and start drinking again, every time thinking it would be different.

During my early twenties, I was diagnosed with rheumatoid arthritis and fibromyalgia. There were times when I couldn't get out of bed or I would end up in the hospital. On days when I felt better, I would pop pain pills and go drinking.

I started going to the clubs on my own because Rob became extremely jealous. When I started to feel suffocated, I would take off on him to drink and cheat. My disease made me feel undesirable and unwanted.

When I researched rheumatoid arthritis online and saw pictures of what it looked like, I would get depressed thinking of how I would become deformed and confined to a wheelchair and no one would want me. I would get sloppy drunk, end up in cars and alleys with strangers, and sometimes I would end up in the back of a cop car and brought home.

Twice during those days, I was mistaken for a prostitute. Once, when I was walking by myself, I got chased by a man who told me he wanted an hour. The second time was at a hotel party with a guy who wanted me to meet up with his well-off white friends. They asked him if I was an escort because I was a Native.

Both times I didn't even question it or make a connection that I was being stereotyped.

I was oblivious about who I surrounded myself with. My best friend at the time, Thomas, was heavily involved in the partying lifestyle, but I didn't pay any attention to it because he kept me away from it. I was so self-involved that I didn't even look around to see what was happening. I had met Thomas at a fitness centre that we both went to. Eventually I started working at the fitness centre and he would visit with me while I was working.

When I asked Thomas what he did for work, he told me he was an art dealer. Rob had grown up with a dad who was a drug dealer and pimp, so he laughed at me when I told him this. He told me that art dealers don't drive Escalades like that or hang out with friends who get flown into parties in a helicopter.

I was hanging out with people who were involved in organized crime, but I had no fear and didn't think about my well-being or safety because I didn't think I was at risk. There were times when I would be around hundreds of thousands if not millions of dollars' worth of drugs and money, and people who were enforcers and dealers. I sat at the table with people who were so high up they wouldn't even touch the money or drugs.

Thomas and I would often sit off to the side in the club and have some deeply intense conversations. I knew he was a brilliant man. We were both living in extremely dark places and really knew nothing about each other. We told each other stories about our lives but we never talked about how we felt about it or how it affected us. Sometimes he would start to ask me questions about why I was so guarded, and we would get into arguments when he tried to push me out of my comfort zone.

I was a violent person and disliked most of the people he surrounded himself with. They were all blond, beautiful people who reminded me of the kids from school. When they would try to interrupt us or get involved in our conversations, I would cut them off or glare at them until they walked away. I was known for my violence, for fighting, and people knew that I would punch someone without warning if they looked at me the wrong way.

Thomas once told me I was the most jaded person he had ever met, and I didn't understand what he meant. He told me I was hiding and wanted to know why I was so angry. He thought I was one of the smartest women he knew and didn't understand why I behaved the way I did. When he talked to me like that, I would stop talking to him for days.

I was always drawn back to him, though. I liked feeling special and knew that he drew people to him from all backgrounds. He had a personality that made you want to be around him. He was good at making you feel like you were important.

Eventually the lifestyle caught up with him and he was indicted for organized crime, the first person in B.C. to be convicted of committing crimes for the benefit of a criminal organization. He was sentenced to a total of ten years. They tried to make it sixteen. We stayed in touch for a few months and he would call to check in until he realized I was starting on a different path. Then the calls stopped.

When Thomas went into prison he didn't have a Grade-12 education, and while he was incarcerated he finished school in order to take university-level writing and criminology. He began talking with the young men who were coming in. He wondered why they were leaving and coming back, and he helped design a program to help young guys stay out of jail. Eventually his work led to an early release and it took me a while before I trusted that he was living a better life.

One of our first visits was doing a workout together at a gym. He caught me up on his experiences and told me he was getting involved in the cannabis and hemp business. I laughed because I thought it was all perfect timing for him, and that the universe must love him.

Since then he has had some humbling moments, but he has used the whole experience to drive himself to succeed in a number of legitimate businesses with businessmen who offered to coach him. He has always been fully open and honest about his past and shares his thoughts openly on how he thinks we can change things, while continuing to mentor young men and keep them out of the jail system.

When Thomas and I were still in our party mode, my boyfriend Rob started to DJ and work security at one the nightclubs in town. He used to get upset with me when the owner of the club would tell me and my sister Wynette to go find people from the other clubs to bring over. In exchange for bringing people in, he tore up my tab at night. It was easy to pretend I had money of my own, because I would buy rounds of shots and run my tabs up to $1,000 a night. People thought I was rich. By the end of the night I would go to the bar for my tab and the bartender would rip it up or light it on fire for me.

I could walk into the club with bikers whose presence took over the room. I thought it was cool that the owner would keep the upstairs section open for us until four in the morning. I felt untouchable, knowing people were scared of the people I was with. I felt safer with them than I had ever felt in the past ten years.

I never did touch hard drugs. In the back of my mind I always felt like if I did, my spirit would leave me and never come back, that I would die a dark death. I thank my mom for her teachings and my grandmother for her stories, because when I was in my darkest hours, hearing their voices in the back of my head kept me alive.

When I was involved in powwow and ceremony, my teachers always told me to take care of my spirit, my outfits, and my feathers. They told me if I drank, my spirit would leave for days and be replaced by the alcohol spirit. That is why people feel hungover and dead inside after drinking.

Those are the things I thought of the next day, lying alone with blankets on the windows and the doors locked so no one would see me or smell the alcohol on my skin, cringing at the thought of everything I had done and said the night before.

7

When I turned twenty-two, I decided I was going to get sober again. After six months of not drinking, I applied for a job with our band health department. I remember sitting in the job interview as they asked me about my wellness plan.

It took me a moment to think and I decided to be honest for once about my six months of sobriety. Even then I had this crazy notion that no one knew about my drinking.

I ended up getting the job and started to work as the receptionist and community health representative. They gave me a giant binder to learn about our health benefits and I was tasked with creating a filing system. I had no experience in any of these areas, but I always figured things out.

We lived in my mom's house on the reserve. People stayed with us here and there; sometimes we had good people who helped with food and gave us money to help with the bills.

Other people came and stayed for the free place to crash, and they would remain as long as they could until I would snap and kick them out. I wasn't good at boundaries, so instead of having conversations with people I went right to unreasonable behaviour and blame. Most of the time people had no idea what had happened. One minute I acted like everything was great and fine and the next minute I ran off a list of things they had done wrong and told them to leave.

Evelyn and I lived in the house together with our boyfriends Nacoma and Rob for a few years, and we went through many hard times. They all trusted me to take care of things around our home, but I had no idea how to be responsible. When I wasn't drinking I did my best to support us, but I had no idea how to handle money once I had it.

We were so used to having nothing that when we did get money we wanted to spend it, and I would end up having to decide which bills I needed to pay that month and which I would let slide for another month or two. We went back and forth between having different services cut off. If we lucked out and managed to get money, we would pay off the phone or internet bill and feel very accomplished when we had our services back.

I always felt responsible for taking care of everyone. After my mom had her stroke, I felt like her responsibilities were left with me, but I wasn't prepared for it.

Before the stroke, my mom made sure that our family was taken care of and that everyone had rides to where they needed to go. If someone called her at work, or if she was busy doing something, she would drop what she was doing to go and help them.

I took on her way of taking care of others. I was a people pleaser, so I always went out of my way to take care of things, even if it meant sacrificing my own time, work and priorities. The worst part about it was that I just did things because I thought they were expected of me. I took on the role of caretaker and just assumed people needed me, without having them ever ask me to do anything for them.

After my mom was moved into a care home, we did our best to visit her whenever we had a vehicle to use and gas money. Sometimes we brought her home for the weekends and holidays. I had so much gratitude for Rob and Nacoma during this time, because they were strong enough to lift my mom and put her in the car and carry her and her wheelchair up and down the stairs in our house. They did this without question, and always found ways to make sure she was comfortable.

By the time Kyle was almost four, his grandmother decided he could come live with us again. She slowly started to bring his stuff to our house. He still spent half his time with his grandma and grandpa, but I felt good knowing she thought he would be okay with me.

We didn't have any money when Kyle moved in with us and I wanted to make his bedroom welcoming, so Rob and I went shopping with the little amount of money I had to buy him sheets and a blanket for his bed.

Rob told me he was going for a walk and would be right back. He came back later and told me to come with him to pick out some bedding sets that I didn't have the money for. He told me that he went to talk to one of the ladies at customer service and they gave him a $500 store credit card.

We were always struggling but felt like we were in much better positions than most of the people around us. We were also proud of ourselves that we were able to do so much on our own because we didn't have families we could turn to and ask for help. In fact, it was often our family members who came to us to ask for help, and we would do what we could with what little we had.

I went through times of depression and mania, moments where I was so sad and low-energy that I couldn't get out of bed. I would spend a lot of time at work on the computer and my wrists started burning and hurting. I went to my doctor and he told me it was probably carpal tunnel syndrome and that I needed a wrist brace.

Soon after, my shoulder started hurting with pain that would last for hours. I would wake up in the morning and feel extremely stiff; it would take me half an hour to an hour to loosen up just to be able to get out of bed.

I started researching my symptoms on the internet and kept seeing the word *arthritis* pop up. I started to worry because I realized that there were many forms of arthritis, and my symptoms seemed to indicate I had one of the worst you could get.

I called my doctor and made another appointment with a full list of symptoms for him. He was hesitant at first and told me he thought I was too young to have the kind of arthritis I was worried about, but I told him about my family history. It was only then that he ordered blood work. A week later I was diagnosed with rheumatoid arthritis.

I was devastated. I remembered my aunts who had joint replacements and surgeries because of their arthritis.

Rheumatoid arthritis is classified as an autoimmune disease, which results in your body attacking itself. With rheumatoid arthritis, white blood cells attack healthy cartilage and break it down. If left untreated, it will cause deformity of the joints. There is no cure for rheumatoid arthritis.

In the first year, my disease spread throughout my body very quickly. I was referred to a rheumatologist with a two-year wait list, but because I was young I was bumped up the list.

My doctor told me he wanted to be aggressive for two reasons: firstly because of my age and secondly because my rheumatoid arthritis blood counts were high, which meant the disease would be ruthless on my body.

He told me he would have to try different medications to see what worked best for me. He also talked about his disappointment in the health coverage offered by Indigenous and Northern Affairs Canada, and mentioned how no other health coverage was as discriminatory as ours. He told me I would have to try different medications that would make me sick so that I could prove these medications weren't working for me. After we had worked through all the cheap and less effective medications, he would then be able to prescribe me the drug that was more expensive but worked the best.

In the beginning, I tried to make it work with the different medications he prescribed, but I was nauseated, sick and in pain all the time, and my inability to move was still there. I lost my energy levels and was constantly depressed. Mornings were the worst, and some days it took me up to two hours to get out of bed, while other days I couldn't get out of bed at all. My physical pain quickly added to my emotional pain and I didn't know how to deal with it.

I couldn't do simple things on my own without feeling pain. Just going to the bathroom and undoing my own pants and buttons was a chore, and I couldn't wear shoes with a heel. I ended up walking down the stairs sideways, holding on to the railing because the pain and swelling in my feet, ankles and knees was so intense.

All of the things that we take for granted every day became almost impossible for me. The worst pain happened in my shoulders and I couldn't lift my arms to even brush my own hair. At the time, I was twenty-two years old and I had a twenty-year-old boyfriend who was willing to be a stepfather to my four-year-old son. Rob was now having to help me in and out of bed, brush my hair and take on much more responsibility for Kyle than he had ever counted on. He was tending to me when I couldn't get out of bed and taking care of my son, feeding him and getting him ready for school.

I constantly questioned why Rob would want to be with me. I didn't think he loved me; I just thought he needed a place to live and so that's why he stayed.

The drinking did nothing to improve my condition. I was constantly in the hospital and eventually ended up taking morphine to help dull the pain. I also started seeking ways to numb my emotions.

My arthritis, drinking and self-destruction took over most of my life in my early twenties. I was angry at my body and angry at myself for being completely incapable of doing anything independently. I spent a lot of time pitying myself and even more so when my arthritis began to affect my chest walls and muscles. The pain was so bad I would think I was having a heart attack. There were times when my arthritis would flare up in my jaw and

I would be in so much pain that I couldn't open my mouth to eat. I thought so many times that Kyle was never going to know me, and I would be dead before I turned thirty.

There were times when I would drug myself up completely just to stop feeling. I started abusing prescription pills; even Tylenol and Advil in high doses helped me numb myself.

When I was drinking, I felt like I had no problems. I had no illness and couldn't feel anything. I had no responsibilities and I felt wanted by people who were out to have a good time. People wanted to party with me, dance with me, and take me home. I got caught up in a circle of people who were heavily involved in the drug scene, which seemed glamorous at the time because we were given special treatment by everyone. While I didn't touch the drugs that were circulating around me, I did feel like I had a place where I belonged.

My life went on like this in a big fuzzy depression. I don't remember half of the things that happened to me during those years. I was so out of it half the time I barely even remembered any of the friendships that I formed.

There were times when we had no money and couldn't even afford Tylenol or Advil. There were times we didn't have food, and in those moments I would call on one of my best friends from childhood, Karen, and her husband Jon. They would bring me medicine and food and check on me to make sure I was okay. Karen was really good at remembering my medical history and was one of the few people I would allow to see me in the hospital.

On a few occasions at home, I would write letters detailing my final wishes and what I wanted if I died. Most of the time it was after I had been in the hospital because of a flareup or a complication with my medication. Once I had stayed in the hospital for a few days with a kidney infection, and another time I was there because they wanted to make sure the pain in my chest wasn't my heart.

One early evening in the fall, I was standing in my kitchen getting ready to take my medication when I heard my boyfriend laughing with Kyle in the front yard. I watched them for a while as they ran around, jumping and wrestling and kicking balls, and I thought to myself, *I will never be able to do that with them. What good am I?* I started thinking of the hundred reasons why I was a horrible mother. I thought of how everyone would be better off without me. I felt like such a burden. I started crying, and while I stood there crying and getting angry I looked at my medication and wondered, *Did I already take my dose?* Then I realized I didn't care and took all of the pills in my cupboard.

I made my way back up to my room and lay down on my bed. Things were getting fuzzy and I faded in and out of consciousness. I felt my heart beating funny and thought, *This is it. I'm dying.* I started to get scared and my anxiety hit. As I started to fade out again, the front door opened and I could hear the boys come in and I heard Kyle's laughter.

The sound of his laughter snapped me back to the world, and I thought to myself, *What am I doing?* I called out for Rob to come upstairs.

He came to my bed and asked me what was up, and I told him what I had done. He asked me if he should phone an ambulance and I told him I didn't want one. In my head I thought about how I didn't want everyone on the reserve to know what I had done. At that moment, I cared more about people's gossip than I did about my own life.

He decided to drive me to the hospital himself. The car didn't have headlights, insurance or gas and it was already getting dark outside, but it was going to get us to where we needed to go.

We got in the car and I held on to Kyle. He was scared because he knew something was wrong with me, but he always kept a cool head, even at that young age. Rob got me to the hospital in the middle of the night and they kept me there.

The next day my rheumatologist came to see me. I burst into tears because I felt so helpless. He looked at me with a serious face and said, "You don't have to live in pain anymore."

Until that moment, I didn't think I would ever be free from pain. I felt like my entire life was pain, but I never complained out loud. Instead, I stayed in bed and suffered in silence, and only those closest to me in my life knew how bad my disease actually was. I suffered in silence because I didn't want to explain myself and I didn't want pity. Most of all, I just wanted to be normal. From the moment I woke up in the morning until the moment I fell asleep every night, I felt pain and discomfort and was limited in what I could do.

Not only did I think of the physical pain I was in, but I was being affected by the emotional pain too, and I had absolutely no idea how to deal with it without going crazy. I promised my doctor and myself that I would start cooperating with him and take my treatment seriously in order to get better, which included taking my medication properly. I wanted to run and play with Kyle and be healthy and alive for him, so that eventually I would be someone he could be proud to call his mom.

Coming out of the hospital, I knew my life had to change and I had to make a commitment to being healthy. At the time, I had no idea what healthy was. I grew up with a mom who always talked about her weight. We grew up on macaroni and cheese, instant noodles and comfort foods. We thought hot dogs were a good protein and that potatoes were a healthy vegetable and there was no such thing as exercise.

I read information on the Arthritis Society's website and did research to educate myself. I eventually decided to make an appointment with a naturopath to see if there were other options I could try that didn't make me feel so sick.

My naturopath tested me for food sensitivities and taught me about acidic and alkaline foods, and "pain foods" that caused inflammation. I started eating less red meat, dairy, white bread, pork and nightshade plants, and I started eating more salad, chicken, carrot sticks and rice. Eventually, I was able to start adding things back into my diet, but it was pretty limited considering I didn't have much money to spend on the kind of diet I really needed.

My naturopath told me I needed to continue taking my medication because there was nothing he could prescribe to me that would stop my joints from degenerating. However, he did let me know about some supplements that would help to protect my liver from damage by the hardcore medications and deal with the inflammation.

One day when I was leaving his office, I stopped to look at a few posters on the tack board. One of them advertised a yoga class to help deal with chronic pain. I had never really heard of yoga or paid any attention to it, but it looked like it might be easy and gentle and something I could do.

I went to my first yoga class and connected with the yogi, who told me which classes I should take for pain management, and taught me modified poses in the class. Yoga was more challenging than I thought it would be, but I started to feel stronger.

There were certain poses I couldn't hold because my arms were too shaky. I felt like I would be able to benefit even more from yoga if I was stronger. So, I went to one of our local gyms and signed up to try things out.

At first I had no idea what I was doing, and it must have showed because one of the personal trainers came up and offered to do a session with me to teach me how to do a proper workout.

The first thing he had me do was jump on the treadmill, and he told me to warm up for ten minutes. The first ten minutes were tough because I was still smoking cigarettes and worried running would be rough on my joints.

After that, every time I went to the gym, I would jump on the treadmill to do a walk or run, and it got easier every time until I was able to run for a full ten minutes. I was also getting more involved with my job and decided I should stop smoking if I was going to work as the receptionist in a health department.

The one thing my mom always stressed to me was the importance of knowing where you are and what you are doing, because there are going to be many times when people will be looking to you as a role model. Because of that, I felt guilty every time I left a staff meeting to have a smoke.

Little by little I started learning about health. I learned about drinking enough water, eating healthy foods, and getting active. I joined and led a community challenge called Honour Your Health, where I learned to take charge of my own well-being.

I read articles, watched videos, and kept talking to people who were involved in healthy living, and I slowly started to feel better. I was successfully managing my pain by paying attention to what I was eating and taking care of my liver, and I had finally found a skin-injection drug that worked for me. It took me a while to get used to it because it was an immune-system-suppressing drug, so I had to be careful about getting sick and being around people who were really ill, but at least the pain was manageable. It was still there, and I'd get flareups that caused me to feel sore, but it wasn't the kind that put me in the hospital anymore.

Eventually, as my life started to come together, I felt like I was stable and ready to reset all parts of my life. By then Rob and I had been together for seven years, and we decided to get married and be a normal family.

8

Neither Rob nor I knew what a normal family was, but we thought we had figured it out and we were always patting ourselves on the back for being much better parents then our parents were to us. We rarely spent time together; the only time we were together was when we were at the gym working out.

When I met him, he was barely nineteen and I was twenty-one. I walked into the bar after leaving my chaotic alcoholic relationship in the States and asked who he was when I saw him dancing with a bunch of guys I grew up with on the reserve.

Immediately, those around me told me he was a punk. He liked to date a bunch of different girls at the same time and he didn't care if anyone knew. I walked up to him and told him that he was coming home with me and he did. I had picked him because I thought he was not interested in a committed relationship, but he ended up at my house every other day.

I found out he was transitioning out of foster care and living with his aunt. He had grown up in foster and group homes and had lived on the street. His dad had kidnapped him out of the hospital and went on the run with him when he was a baby. His dad was a drug dealer and pimp who was always running from city to city with him to stay away from the cops.

Rob told me stories of all the abuse he endured growing up. He had suffered from sexual and physical abuse. His dad had left so many scars on him from horrific abuse that I couldn't believe Rob was alive.

He told me two things saved him while he was growing up: basketball and hip hop. He grew up with gangs surrounding him in East Vancouver and lived in the Raymur Project on the fringes of the infamous Downtown Eastside. He told me he would wander around downtown and the streetworkers helped to take care of him. He had witnessed people overdosing on his couch and watched someone stab his dad in front of him.

He stayed with his dad until he was in grade school. One day, his friend patted him on the back and notice that he winced in pain. His friend asked him what was wrong with him and he showed his friend his back, which was black and blue from a beating his dad had given him. A few days later, there were cop cars outside of his school and they took him away.

He shared many stories like this, and yet he loved his dad fiercely. His dad eventually got clean and went on to get his certificate for counselling. He worked for the Salvation Army helping street people in Edmonton. They ended up becoming very close and his dad encouraged him to continue telling their story.

Rob was a great performer. He would often do shows for free because they offered him free drinks or exposure. I finally decided to check out one of his shows and stood at the back. As I looked around the room watching people, I realized a majority of them were there to see Rob perform and they were paying cover fees to get in the door.

When we got home that night, I explained to him that he needed to get a contract for his performances, and when he told me he didn't know how I told him I would do it. I wrote out all his contracts, riders and agreements and ended up becoming his manager. Together with my brother-in-law Nacoma, we built our first company and became one of the first Indigenous hip hop crews in Canada.

Back then even my sister Evelyn was rapping. One night we sat at the kitchen table trying to figure out a name for the group.

We were throwing things out there, and Ev finally said, "What about 7th Generation?"

That was it, they became 7th Generation, and we started our first company and called it "Kiqwilly Productions and Entertainment." We derived Kiqwilly from the word *kekuli*, which means "underground house." They were determined to be underground artists who honoured and respected the culture of hip hop and its origins of storytelling, and to bring awareness to the current situation and reality in Indigenous communities.

In 2001 we received an anonymous donation from a woman in the city we lived in because she had read an article about Rob in the local newspaper. The money paid for his studio time. While everyone else was still performing in bars and clubs in their respective cities, we started burning our own CDs and took them to powwows to sell. We made enough money at the powwows to get our CDs professionally pressed.

I knew that he had an amazing story to tell, so I told him we had to get him running workshops and speaking to kids about his life. Through my experience growing up at powwows, going to conferences, and taking the Honour Your Health challenge, I had learned all about conference coordinating. We took all of our combined skills to create a team that worked well together: me with my experience in planning and coordinating, Rob with his ability to sell anything, and Nacoma's technical experience and drive to find ways to get things done.

Rob had an amazing ability to talk to people and connect with them. He could sell anything. I was constantly afraid to approach people because of my fear of rejection; he had no such fear. He had developed skills on the street to survive and people would help him or support him because he had an energy about him that drew people in.

Nacoma had gone to school to be a sound technician and learned how to produce music. He had technical experience and a business sense, and he understood that it took time and personal investment and sacrifice in order to get things done. He wasn't afraid of risk and working hard.

I was the type of person who could learn quickly through reading and research. I watched videos and read articles in business and hip hop magazines. I learned all about the music industry and marketing strategies. I also learned about artist management and promotions and how to write contracts and make travel arrangements.

It was times like those that I heard my mom talking to me in the back of my mind, saying that people could make money doing almost anything, and that all people needed to know was a little bit about everything.

When my mom and I took our long drives, she would look at the baby's breath growing along the roads and say, "I bet if you picked that baby's breath and brought it to a florist, they would buy it from you." Her mind was always thinking like that, and she constantly shared her thoughts with others aloud, never keeping them to herself.

Our hip hop company did really well. Even though Rob and I weren't great with money, we were able to pay most of our bills. Nacoma did the best out of all of us, because he was good at saving money and saying no.

We were in our early twenties and committed to learning everything we needed to know about our roles. I read about music, hip hop, marketing, and management. Eventually, I got into marketing and promotions and started managing other entertainers.

Rob released a number of CDs and even had a music video air on MuchMusic's RapCity. The exposure had him travelling all over Canada. He collaborated with artists like Moka Only from Swollen Members and Darryl McDaniels from Run DMC.

We lived in a small city that rarely supported anyone in the arts, let alone hip hop. We had to deal with racist attitudes and comments about the style of music. No one wanted to rent us their venues because they were afraid we would vandalize them. We had to work extra hard to find ways to promote and market ourselves to get into cities that were dominated and supported by hometown crews.

The entertainment industry is really cliquey. If you aren't close with individuals or in with their crews it's really difficult to get invited to events, and often times we had to invite ourselves in. Most of our support started to come from artists outside of the Indigenous music circles, and it wasn't until Rob started to really move forward on his own that other Indigenous artists started to pay attention.

I learned how normalized drinking and drugs are in the music industry. We also learned how quickly gang members, drug dealers and illegitimate businessmen were willing to invest in a hip hop crew. Afterparties were a big deal at music industry events, along with violence of every sort. We did our best to stay away from it, and eventually I started to stay away from travelling with them, but I knew the lifestyle and wanting to be accepted was attractive to Rob and his extroverted personality.

We worked opposite hours and he travelled on the road, performing and doing workshops for youth all over the country. I was happy with where we were at in our relationship, and I would boast about how independent we were living our own lives and not telling each other what to do. I came to the conclusion I loved him and wanted to spend the rest of my life with him. It was more of a decision in my mind than a feeling in my heart.

I wasn't sure what love was, but I really felt like I was the luckiest person I knew. I was the last person anyone thought would ever get married. I didn't believe in soulmates or everlasting love. While I didn't trust any men in my life, over the years and after all the abuse we put on each other I knew that I could always count on Rob, and he knew that he could always count on me. To us, that was more stability than we had ever had in our lives. Never once did I think it would end. I saw myself growing old with him because, despite our dysfunction, we were best friends. No one else in the world knew our ugliness like we did, but we still found ways to see the best in each other.

Our marriage was rough during the first year. We argued about all the same things we had fought about in the past, and those same issues kept coming up. We both travelled so much, and our careers started to pick up to the point where we only saw each other five days out of the month.

He spent his time as a performer and motivational speaker. I was still his manager, but I was also an intern for the provincial government of British Columbia and travelled all over the province. Sometimes we would be in an airport at the same time and never even see each other.

It was during this time that I also decided to run for chief of the Penticton Indian Band. I felt that I was capable and understood leadership. I went to visit people in the community to listen to their thoughts and concerns. I had spent most of my time in support roles and always behind the scenes of our company, and I know that Rob struggled because my attention was focused on something other than him.

Time went by and I knew our relationship was getting rough; we couldn't even sleep in the same room anymore. I was one year sober, and I made a decision in October 2009 to go to a personal development seminar. Rob was completely against it because a group of his friends refused to go. He told me he would rather go to some kind of treatment centre than to a personal development seminar. We both knew we had a lot of stuff to deal with, and I knew that if I was the only one working toward healing I was going to leave him behind, but I was desperate not to be alone.

As the time drew near for him to go to the trauma treatment centre, I started to worry. We met in between one of his shows and one of my meetings and he cried so hard that I started to cry with him. I held him in my arms and told him it was going to be okay. He had so much hurt and memories coming up he didn't know what to do or how he was supposed to feel.

The next day we all got ready to go our separate ways. Rob met up with his crew and they took off for the airport on their way to the Canadian Aboriginal Music Awards in Toronto. It was an award show they had striven to be a part of their entire music career. This was the one they had wanted to win for years. My sisters and I were very excited for them, even though we had to drive five hours back home to attend something before driving back to the city the next day to attend yet another meeting.

On our way back into the city I received a text message that said, "We Won!" I was stuck in traffic with my sisters, so we called them up to congratulate them. He had just won the award and was getting ready to go on stage to perform, so I let him go, telling him I would see him when I picked him up from the airport the next day.

It was then he did something I never thought he would do. He left his crew, rented a room with a woman who was his backup dancer, and forever changed not only his life, but all of our lives as we knew them.

After my meetings in the city that day, I made my way out to the airport with my family. We saw Rob and his crew proudly pull out their award as they come down the escalator. There was nothing different about my husband, and I didn't suspect anything at all. The boys in his crew left on their own and Rob came with my sisters and me.

We left the city later in the day and the roads became really scary because of winter weather. We were all very tired so we ended up pulling over and spending the night at a halfway point. It was a horrible evening because I was mad, tired and scared. I screamed at him for snoring because I was so exhausted and told him to sleep on the floor. We woke up early because we knew we would have to get back home in time for Rob to meet up with his counsellor and head off to the treatment centre.

When we got home, we stayed in our room as he started to pack, and he talked about making it through this tough time. From my perspective everything was going well, which is crazy to me now because it was insanity at the time. In my crazy and co-dependant head, I had a perfect husband and a perfect marriage. While our marriage had its rough points, we felt that we were invincible as he left for his six-week treatment program.

I was always exhausted. I was working a job I didn't believe in anymore and running for council in my community, but I wasn't even sure I wanted to commit to it. I did it because I had run for chief, didn't win, and made a promise to community members who voted for me that I would run for council.

One day in early December, I received a phone call from the treatment centre saying my husband had checked out days before and they were following up to see if he had made it home. It only took a day to travel from the treatment centre back home and so my mind went from being upset to angry to worried. I tried to call and text him, with no response. Twice he answered and hung up, so I knew that something was going on. I left a voicemail asking him to let me know that he was okay.

I left my meeting early; I was upset and angry with my supervisors for a number of reasons and I had a forty-five-minute drive home. I was completely preoccupied with trying to find my husband.

I wondered if I had just quit my job and I also knew I had to go to our election later that evening. I was tired, and I knew as soon as the results were in I would have to leave right away and drive for five hours for a meeting the next day, and I was only going to get three hours of sleep.

An hour before I walked into the elections, I sent Rob a text telling him I knew where he was, even though I didn't. I told him I was going to get on the next plane I could and fly there. I received a text from him, and it only had three short sentences: "It's done. We're over. I hate you."

I called my sister Wynette into my room and showed her the message. I started to cry. She sat next to me and held me, and I told her we had to go. I got my stuff together and we walked out the door to head down to the elections at the community hall. There was no way I could miss the elections; I felt it would be too disrespectful to the people who had nominated me and the people who supported me. This is a solid example of how I used to put other people's ideas and expectations over my own health and well-being.

I sat in my vehicle and pulled myself together. I walked into the building and no one had a clue what was happening with me. I sat in the corner, not wanting to talk to anyone. I wondered if they knew how much pain I was in or if it showed on my face.

Everyone was bent over their tally sheets, listening for the counts, writing names down and trying to predetermine who the winners were going to be. I looked at my sister and whispered to her that I wanted to leave, as I felt like I couldn't breathe and that an anxiety attack was coming on. She didn't understand why we didn't just leave in the first place.

In my mind, I didn't want to leave because I didn't want people to think I was walking out for other reasons. The votes were being split between me and three other people for the last seat on council, and I didn't want anyone to think I was acting self-important. I sat there telling myself that I would not cry until I got back into the van.

As the night drew to a close, I breathed a sigh of relief as I heard the results. My name wasn't called so I was free to run out. The one person besides my sister who knew what was happening stopped me as I was leaving and asked, "How are you doing?"

His look of concern busted down my wall and tears started streaming down my face. This man, the community counsellor, a family friend, an uncle to me, held me while I cried and told him how my husband had left me.

It was that moment that people started to line up behind me, wanting to hug me and tell me, "It's okay sweetie, you do a good job, you'll get a spot in the next election." I just nodded and said thank you.

Wynette drove me home to grab my things. It was eleven p.m. and we had a five-hour drive in the snow ahead of us. I had a meeting the next morning and didn't want to miss it. As I packed my stuff and came down the stairs, I looked at my thirteen-year-old and Wynette's fifteen-year-old son and said, "You guys want to come with us?"

I didn't want to go on the trip without Kyle, and I knew I had to tell him what happened right away. I sat down beside him and told them I had something to tell them. I drew in a deep breath, looked into his eyes and said, "He's gone. He's left and he's not coming back. I didn't want you to find out from anyone else." As I looked at the boys, their eyes filled with tears. Wynette and I held our sons as they cried. They had no idea why he would leave us. It wasn't just me whom Rob had left, it was all of us. We all wanted him to come home and we were heartbroken because we couldn't figure out why he wasn't.

We slowly packed our things into the vehicle and got on the road. We didn't know what to think, and I didn't want to talk about it. I just wanted to be numb and not feel the pain I felt. In one moment I couldn't figure out what I did wrong, and in the next I had a dozen reasons.

The meeting I attended the next day ended up being a session about multigenerational trauma. I had to listen to what trauma meant, as I didn't really know what it was. The facilitators shared a list of experiences that cause trauma, and although I saw myself in the list I kept thinking of Rob.

After the meeting, Wynette drove while I sat in the front seat and texted him. Every day after that I told myself I wouldn't text him, but every day I found something else to say to him, hoping he would change his mind. I told him I was sorry for pushing him, that I wanted to explain to him what I had learned about trauma and how I hoped he would forgive me. He never did text back unless it was to tell me how much he hated me and how happy he was without me in his life.

As Wynette drove us back home, I asked my nephew to sit in the front seat so I could lie in the back and cry, hoping Kyle wouldn't hear me because he was too involved in his video games. I didn't want him to know how badly I was hurting, but he turned around and grabbed my hand. He rubbed it and looked at me. I could see in his eyes that he wanted to take the pain away.

We got home, and I went right to my room and laid in bed for days. I stopped eating. I suffered from insomnia and slipped into a deep depression. My husband told people we had a mutual agreement to separate. I told myself that I deserved this heartache for all the wrong I had done in my life and was convinced this was karma.

My spirit, heart, mind and body all broke on the same day. It wasn't the first time it all fell apart in my life, but it was going to be the first time that I dealt with my pain while staying sober. I felt every raw and gut-wrenching emotion. I felt all the pain, heartache, and body aches. I slipped into a place that I didn't know existed for myself. I remember seeing women get depressed and sad over men and telling myself, "That will never be me."

I was the type of person to run away. I would drink away the pain or I would find empty companionship to make me feel like I was filling the void, soothing the pain and numbing the aches that I felt in my spirit.

I cried for hours. I couldn't eat or sleep, and I would get angry, sad and delirious all at the same time. People told me, "Time will heal and take care of you." People sent me great reminders of my strength, and it was those things that kept me going.

I woke up every morning to smudge and say prayers for healing and love and hope to get through the day. I prayed for myself, for Kyle and for Rob.

I had a lot of time to think. Rob and I had a relationship that was unhealthy and toxic. We were both hurting human beings who experienced abuse, trauma and pain.

It wasn't until a full two weeks after my husband had told me it was over that I found out that he had cheated on me while he was in Toronto at the music awards, and he had planned to leave me as soon as he got home. The trauma treatment centre was in Cranbrook and she was in Edmonton. She bought him a bus ticket from Cranbrook to Edmonton within days of him getting there. He only spent three days in the treatment centre before checking himself out.

Like any insane and jilted wife, I reached out to her and asked her if she knew that he was married with a family. She responded by telling me things about myself that only my husband knew, which let me know he had told her everything about me.

He told her that he had been unloved, and that he was miserable. Not only did he walk out, but he broke something sacred by telling a stranger every vulnerable thing about me and our relationship.

I harassed her and sent her hate mail. I found ways to attack her and the way she looked and dressed. I found every way possible to send her notes to let her know what an awful person she was. Not knowing her at all, not knowing her story, I only wanted her to hurt as much as I was hurting.

He continued to be very public with her and acted like it was okay. It took me a while to realize he wasn't coming back. I finally gave up and told myself I didn't care.

Every day I kept thinking that he still loved me and that he would get over this phase in his life, that he would come back to me and I would forgive him and still love him and put it all behind us. I became very desperate. I didn't want to lose him or be alone, and I knew that if I kept on like this I was going to go crazy.

I didn't understand just how unhealthy and co-dependant I was at the time. People couldn't understand why I would want him back. In my mind I kept thinking of how much he needed me. I felt like I could save him from himself because I was the only one who really knew him.

I didn't know he had started drinking long before he cheated on me. He would buy a bottle of alcohol and sneak it back to his room and drink by himself so no one would know. I heard he might have been getting involved in drugs and I couldn't imagine how hurt he was to go that far. He was hanging out with a Native gang in Edmonton who had become one of the most prominent gangs in Canada. They were known for drugs, violence and prostitution.

I turned to one of my adopted moms, who was a pipe carrier and sundancer. She told me I had to start waking up before the sun came up when the pipe carriers sent their prayers out. She told me to light sage and take it out and pray to the four directions and to pray for myself, for my son and for Rob.

We planned to have a *yuwipi* healing ceremony after Christmas. My mom Sophie was really involved in yuwipi, and she hosted many yuwipis with people she trusted from South Dakota.

It was a ceremony that involved a lot of preparation and protocols. I prepared my offerings for the altar and then spoke to the yuwipi man and told him what was happening to my husband. I told him I didn't think Rob was thinking clearly because he was lost in his alcoholism and addictions and trauma and he had cut off all communication with us. I prayed for his safety and for his mind to be cleared. We were told that because Rob was so public and doing things he shouldn't be doing, someone had decided to teach him a lesson and put something over his third eye to stop him from seeing.

We went into ceremony, and as we sang and prayed. Ceremony is a time to focus and pray. Often new people don't know, and sometimes they even start to talk while in ceremony because they do not know what they're supposed to be doing.

It is during this time that you listen, pay attention, and pray and practice discipline and focus on all the reasons you are there.

This ceremony is conducted in darkness and all light from windows and doors is blacked out with blankets, black garbage bags and duct tape, because the spirits will get distracted by the light. We are told not to bring electronics, jewellery, or anything else that might be shiny.

The singers have drums and they sing songs and the altar comes alive. The altar is where the yuwipi man sits, wrapped in blankets as he talks to the ancestors, the spirits, the grandfathers and grandmothers.

Sometimes you can see the spirits dancing and hear them chattering; sometimes you will see flashes of light. Other times you will hear and feel eagles flying by your face, blessing you. It feels very supernatural, and most times people want to question if it is real or a trick.

At this particular ceremony, I was there with Kyle. We were sitting in the dark. It was very crowded and there was no way that anyone could get up and walk around without stumbling or tripping over someone else.

As the singing stopped, the yuwipi man asked me to stand up in the dark to get doctored by the spirits for my husband. I stood up and waited. The yuwipi man asked me if I felt anything and I replied no. Kyle then spoke up and said, "I did."

The spirits or ancestors, the rock people, decided to doctor my son instead because of his good heart. He didn't hold the same emotions, manipulations or dysfunction I did. They told us our prayers had been heard and Rob would be fine.

We finished the ceremony as we finish most ceremonies: we had a feast. Yuwipis always begin after the sun goes down and end around ten or eleven p.m.

It was near midnight when we finally loaded up our stuff, thanked everyone for their help, and went out to our vehicle to head back to our hotel room in the city. I was in the middle of giving Kyle a blanket and pillow for the trip when my cellphone rang.

It was Rob. I stood there for a minute, not believing it. I answered the phone and he very casually said hello and asked what I was doing. I told him we just got out of ceremony. He told me that he just wanted to phone to see how things were, and he wanted to let me know he was okay and thinking of coming back to B.C.

It was a short call but one that filled me with a sense of relief. At that point I didn't care if he came back to me, I just wanted him to be okay.

On New Year's Day, he phoned me to tell me that he had made mistakes and wanted to be friends. I found out she had kicked him out, but I was still hoping that we would find a way to reconcile. He said he didn't want a divorce and would rather just be separated.

He tried to get me to agree that I knew it was over a long time ago. In the back of my mind, I told myself that I would be a strong and faithful wife. I would find ways to let him know that I still loved him and would still be there for him. I kept thinking about how he had been through so much hurt and pain, and as soon as he snapped out of it we'd work it out.

It wasn't long after that he asked me for his clothes and some money for a plane ticket back to B.C., and I said yes. A week later he told me he never loved me and only married me because he thought it would make him love me more.

When he returned to B.C., he continued to drink and run around in nightclubs with different girls. I thought back to how we had met and realized that he had reverted back to the same broken kid, still on the run. He just wanted to find someone to love him.

I found out that my registration for a personal development program called Choices had been accepted and paid for as part of my new job. At the time Choices was based in Abbotsford, B.C., and I was excited and scared all at the same time.

I left my house and went to visit people who told me I didn't have to make excuses for this man any longer and I didn't deserve the way I was treated. They told me, "You can do this on your own." I made a decision to quit making people feel pity for his anguish, and to start to care about myself more than him.

9

The day I left for Choices, I had no idea what to expect. I read on their website, "You cannot heal or change what you do not acknowledge." I was terrified because I knew there were so many things in my life I couldn't acknowledge.

I didn't know if I could handle it, but I decided I was going to make the entire experience about me and not him and what I could do to make him heal. I wanted to know peace and happiness. I wanted to let go of my anger.

It was the scariest thing I have ever done in my life. But when it came down to it, as scared as I was I stood up and participated and shared, even when it felt like I was being ripped to shreds.

I was real. I shared everything that ever hurt me as a child and as an adult, and I realized not once in my life had I ever really cried for myself, not even when my husband left. I cried for him and all the pain he must have been feeling that made him act the way he was.

For the first few days, I sat there and participated and shared parts of myself, but I didn't cry. This withholding of emotion surprised people in the room, especially when I talked about some of the hurts and pains in my life.

There was a point when they asked me what my greatest shame was, and that was the moment I started to cry. Nothing came out because I felt so much shame. Shame for things I had done to others, for things I had done to myself, and for things done to me. I couldn't pick just one greatest shame because I had so many.

At one point in the Choices program, we were required to give feedback on each other. When it was my turn, some people said they experienced me as a doormat, others told me they thought I was being fake because I put all this work into helping others but I didn't do anything to help myself. This process was hard for many people in the room, but I took it all with little emotion. It wasn't until someone said they experienced me as an abandoned little girl that I finally broke down crying.

In the evenings, after long and emotional days, we would check in with our seminar buddies and talk about what came up for us, but there was no small talk. They were all deep and meaningful conversations where we were able to share who we truly were.

Near the end of the Choices program, the facilitators asked me, "What do you want more of in life?" and I immediately said I wanted to be happy.

They asked me what happy looked like, and I told them that I didn't know because I had never really been happy. They asked me about certain times in my life and to explain what it felt like, and I told them I didn't know, that I'd merely guessed I'd felt happy.

I started to get frustrated because I didn't know what answer they wanted from me. They ended up calling in one of the experienced coaches. She looked at me and asked what I felt like the day I got married.

I laughed and said I didn't know. I was upset with her because she knew what happened to my marriage. I intentionally hadn't mentioned it once throughout the training because I didn't want that to be the focus of my story.

Then she asked me what I felt like the day my son was born. I could feel my face fall and my head get dizzy. I wanted to run from the room and drop to my knees. I stood there, not sure what to say. I tried to dive deep into my mind to find out what that feeling was, and got scared because I couldn't find anything.

I didn't realize that the answer I was looking for wasn't in my head but stored in my heart, and it had been a really long time since I had been there.

After standing there crying for what felt like forever, she asked me if it was love that I felt. I said I didn't know, so she asked me, "When was the last time you felt love? When was the last time you felt safe as a little girl?"

I knew exactly what moment I felt safe and loved. It was when I would lie at night with my tema and she would rub my back and tell me stories. I felt safe and loved, and I felt it in my heart. I couldn't remember the last time I'd had that feeling.

I thought of Kyle and the feeling I had for him, and when they asked me what I wanted more of in my life, I said that I wanted love. I began to understand that in order to feel love I would have to learn to love myself.

There is something everyone can benefit from when reading self-help books and learning about loving yourself or healing yourself. It is something completely different to stop and take the time to talk about what you are thinking and feeling with others, even if you are afraid of what they will say.

When I got home after attending Choices, I made a promise that I would love myself and pay attention to nurturing everything about me. I would nurture my relationship with Kyle, and I would feel this joy, this happiness and peace in everything I did. I would work hard at what I had learned, and I would never go back to that place that left me feeling insecure and needing to be in control, as I now realized that this behaviour no longer served me well and had always made me unhappy.

The night I got home, Evelyn and Wynette and my son and nephew all saw the difference in me right away. For years I had walked around with a straight face and constantly condemned, judged and criticized everyone and everything, and I never took accountability for anything in my life. I was always the first one to blame others. I rarely smiled, I was always serious, and unless I was drinking, I don't remember being fun.

I had so many bad habits that strained my relationships. I didn't know how to ask for what I wanted because I was always so afraid that people would say no or reject me, so I found ways to get what I wanted by manipulating or leading them to where I wanted so that I didn't have to come right out and ask for their help.

If people wanted to do something that I didn't want to do or agree with, I would shame them into doing something else. If they went ahead anyway and did what I didn't want them to do, I would get upset with them and act rude for a few weeks until I forgot about it.

I did all of these things without knowing I was doing them, when all I truly wanted was quality time with people. Most of all I wanted love, but I didn't know how to get it or feel it. Only after I learned to push past my old thinking and fear of being vulnerable was I able to start building some real and genuine relationships with my family. My old beliefs told me that being vulnerable and asking for help was weak.

Rob continued to date one girl after another, many of whom I heard about and knew. I would hear about his partying and self-destructive behaviour. Whenever he would check in with me he would tell me how happy he was feeling. I was okay with that, and I was okay with not seeing him.

It was about three months after Rob and I had separated that Kyle started going through some hard times at school. He was showing a lot of anger and I knew he was more affected than I had originally thought. I reached out to Rob and he agreed to see me to discuss finalizing our separation agreement and spending time with Kyle. I had just finished the second part of my Choices experience and had learned about dealing in the present. I learned about forgiveness and making amends.

As I drove down to meet Rob, I mentally prepared myself to see him. I wasn't going to let him rob me of my newfound happiness and take away everything I had worked so hard to have. I wasn't going to get angry and yell or manipulate him like I used to, and I was going to maintain my sense of independence and freedom.

When I drove up to the restaurant where I was meeting him, I pulled out a gift I had in my pocket and held on to it. In the past I would have been furious, angry, and verbally and physically abusive to someone who had hurt me badly, but that behaviour didn't work for me and I knew it.

As Rob walked around the corner and I saw him, I was reminded that it was the first time seeing him since he had left, humiliated, and hurt me. I wasn't fazed, and I reached up to him to give him a hug. I put my gift in his hand and told him, "I think you are a man worthy of love and forgiveness."

I didn't recognize him anymore, this man I had known for nine years. He had shaved his face and head and he had new piercings, but what shocked me the most was that he had put on so much weight. He was pale and bloated, sickly looking, and he smelled like he had been drinking. His eyes were dull and lifeless. He looked angry and lost but determined to act as if everything was all right.

We sat down for dinner. He told me that I looked different, and simply said, "So you went to Choices."

I was never a big believer in any type of program that claimed to work miracles, and Rob was someone who completely rebelled. He turned his back on anything that involved self-development or digging into something he didn't want to look at, because in his eyes he was fine. But he noticed a difference in me from the moment he saw me, and I told him that I still believed in him regardless of what he had done to hurt me.

He cried, he got mad, and he acted really happy. His mannerisms changed from boyish to stern and angry, from speaking softly to using harsh slang. I spoke to five different personalities that evening, and realized I no longer knew the person in front of me.

He signed our separation agreement and made a promise to himself that he would stay sober. He also mentioned as he left that he would go to Choices too if he had the money.

I walked away feeling proud for believing in myself and for loving myself, for not losing control and knowing I had made the right decision to move on with my life because he wasn't ready to move forward with anyone, let alone himself.

A couple months would pass, and he would continue to drink, travel, meet women and do shows against his better judgment. But we would meet a couple of times over the next few months and each time I would offer him a little bit of support to let him know he was still loved regardless of what he was doing.

It's always hard to pinpoint the moment we started negotiating our marriage, but it got to the point where we agreed to do our best to make it work as long as he made commitments to work on his own happiness.

Reconciling is a test of looking honestly at yourself and not the other person. Forgiveness comes every day. Some days were easier than others, and some days felt like there was none at all. There are constant reminders of the pain, but the best thing I learned through my experience was that my emotions belong to me, and only me. I cannot blame anyone for my emotions except myself.

I still believe that leaving me was the best thing my husband ever did for our marriage.

Without him I couldn't blame anyone else for where I was at, and I was left with myself for the first time in my entire life. I was left to deal with all my toxicity and had to be responsible for my own relationships.

Living with me hadn't been easy because I was quick to judge and point fingers. When Rob left I found freedom, and freedom to me has meant that I have complete control over my life and my emotions, the good and the bad, regardless of what anyone else does or says to me.

10

After six months of working through seminars and counselling and AA meetings, Rob and I recommitted to our marriage and I became pregnant. Kyle was fifteen at the time.

We went to meetings twice a week, sometimes even three. To make our marriage work, we were constantly involved in talking out our issues and being honest with what we were feeling and how we were behaving.

As we worked through it, the founder of Choices, Thelma Box, told us that, "If you want to get out of this marriage, you have to earn your way out. That means doing everything you can to make it work, and if it still doesn't work, you can walk away without blaming each other or blaming yourselves."

We worked through our marriage, but by the time I was six months pregnant I felt that we had rushed back into it without waiting for the glow of the Choices experience to wear off.

We talked honestly about how we didn't feel in love but had love for each other, and agreed it was even awkward to be together. We had moved into separate rooms and were now just living in the same house.

We agreed that we could probably do this for the rest of our lives. We had been through so much together and we were all we knew. We bonded through our trauma, sobriety, and our healing, but when we were honest with ourselves we realized we weren't in love with each other.

When our daughter was born in March, we already had a name for her. We had read a book by Elizabeth Lesser called *Broken Open*, and there was an excerpt that stayed with me that talked about what the author called the Phoenix Process to health and well-being, and how the phoenix would renew itself every five hundred years. She said that everyone was the phoenix, and that we could reproduce ourselves from the shattered pieces of a difficult time and be reborn.

When I finished reading it to Rob, I told him I believed the passage was us. I told him our baby was brought here and born out of a beautiful awakening and self-discovery. Girl or boy, we would name the baby Phoenix.

After she came into the world, my husband and I stayed together until Phoenix was three years old. I started working and travelling again, and Rob stayed home and did shows once a month. He loved being a dad, and his daughter was his world. He was committed to making sure she would never have the kind of life we had growing up.

I constantly felt guilty for travelling so much. Phoenix was active in dancing and swimming and soccer, and Rob made sure she was always involved in something. There were times when he was late or forgot to pack the right food, and sometimes her hair wasn't brushed, but she had no shortage of love in her life.

I would make sure that my flights brought me home as soon as possible, or I would drive just to make it home to put her to sleep or wake up with her. I thought I was an amazing mom. I had a great career and my health was at its best. I felt good about myself but I was never home, and as my daughter got older I knew she wanted to have her mommy around.

When I became busy with work I started to slip into my old behaviours, and I became resentful. I was tired of giving to everyone and I was tired of not getting anything back, but I knew I couldn't share those feelings out loud because I felt that it was stuff that I needed to deal with on my own. I could feel myself shutting down. New things were coming up for me and I had an urge to drink.

Rob knew I was struggling and talked to the friends he had been coached with at the Choices seminar. They put together enough money to send me to a week-long program for my birthday.

I thought I would be prepared this time. I thought I had it all figured out and I had healed—I just needed to take some time for myself. I had no idea I was still hiding under a layer of junk.

When I received feedback from my peers, they called me Martyr Theresa. I had to figure that out and sit with the word *martyr* for a while. What I got stuck on was "a person who voluntarily suffers."

At first, I tried to hide behind my beliefs and make excuses. I believed I had no choice but to put others ahead of me and sacrifice myself, because I was blessed and I felt guilty for having more than others. I didn't want people to think I had an ego, and I never wanted to seem like I felt I was above anyone else.

I thought that I had the tools and discipline to let things go and not let them bother me. I would let things slide instead of having conflict. I didn't like it when people were upset with me, and I didn't think it was a big deal to let another person's comfort be more important than my own if it didn't bother me. I learned that by doing this I was also holding myself back from the things I wanted to do, and so my dreams, ambitions, wants and needs were always put on hold while I tended to the needs and comforts of others.

When I got home, I had some hard discussions with my family. I told them what I needed and what bothered me. Some of what I shared was healing for both parties, because they had no idea I felt that way.

Others told me that not once did they ever ask me to do anything for them and they had no expectations. I had a hard time accepting that, because in my mind I was sure they expected me to take care of them. In the end I realized I was making assumptions, and it humbled me to realize just how many things I assumed and how much those assumptions drove my actions in putting these assumed needs and wants before my own real priorities.

The final talk I had to have was with Rob. He was heading out to a show in the Yukon and I told him we needed to have a good talk when he got home. He said we might as well just do it now.

I asked him if he really wanted to be in a relationship where there was no love, no physical touch and no passion. I asked him if he was okay just being in each other's spaces for the rest of our lives. I asked him, "Don't you ever want to be held and loved?"

That question made him stop and think. He realized that it was something he wanted but was willing to let it go so that our daughter could have both parents. I told him about how I had learned that all our daughter needed was two parents who loved her and loved each other, but that didn't mean we had to be together.

We left it there and he went to the Yukon. When he got back, he agreed with me that we needed to separate but asked if he could have some time to get on his feet, and I agreed. Neither of us were ready to get into a relationship, and so we were okay with sharing the house and getting ourselves ready to separate in a way that didn't leave either of us struggling.

We were pretty level-headed at the time. I give a lot of credit to our commitment to meetings and counselling, and I also know it made a huge difference that neither of us were in a relationship, so we were able to work things out just between the two of us.

We said we would both stay in the house until our bills and joint debts were paid off, and then we agreed we would spend time getting Phoenix used to having only one of us in the house at a time.

One week he would stay in the house and I would leave, and when I came home for a week he would leave. Eventually we agreed it was time for him to move out, and it was extremely scary for both of us. I really didn't want him to leave and there were moments when I asked myself if I was doing the right thing. I wondered if I could make myself love him in a way he needed before realizing that, again, I was trying to make something work for other people and not myself.

He finally moved into an apartment and I helped him furnish it to make it cozy. I spent time with him and Phoenix there until she was okay with the transition. I think it was one of the most heartbreaking things we ever had to do.

We went through ups and downs through our separation, and things always got complicated when we started dating because it added another dynamic to our lives. Falling in love and having a crush on someone definitely changes the way you make decisions. I learned it's never a good idea to communicate with someone when they are in the honeymoon phase.

When someone starts falling in love, all they can think about is the person they are with and when they can be together. This is even more extreme for people who grew up with addictions and alcoholism. There is always a great need to want to be together, and sometimes other priorities can slide.

I say this for both of us, because neither of us knew how to be in a healthy relationship. Trying to make a new relationship work and maintain a healthy alliance with a co-parent and child was almost impossible at times.

We had to work through our co-parenting agreement a few times whenever new people came into the picture, but in the end we always made it work. We made sure to capture our agreements with each other on paper when we were in a good place and in a good frame of mind to remind us of what was important.

When I was home, Phoenix still spent a lot of time with her dad, because he loved to be active with her and he took her out to do fun things with our friends and their children. They both loved to be around people, but I was someone who had to work myself up to being in public with a group, so I stayed home by myself a majority of the time.

Being alone meant that I was able to start taking better care of myself. I was going to the gym more often and I was in the best shape of my life. I had an appointment with my rheumatologist and was told that I was in complete remission from my rheumatoid arthritis and no longer needed to be on medication.

When people ask me how I overcame rheumatoid arthritis, I tell them it's a long story. People often want to know what they can do within a short period of time to heal themselves, but my journey of healing my physical body took me ten years of work.

I had to learn how to take care of my body by paying attention to the junk I was putting into it. I had to stay active and listen to my doctors when it came to taking my medication as directed.

I had to learn to pay attention to how I reacted to my medication, and I had to learn how to communicate with my doctors. I had to trust that they were trying to help me.

All of those things helped me with my pain management. This meant my rheumatoid arthritis wasn't gone, but I was able to manage my pain through medications and proper food and exercise. It was difficult, because I had to learn how to eat healthy on a very limited budget and I had to prioritize food in my life over shopping for other things I needed.

In order to accomplish all of the seemingly simple tasks of communicating, exercising and eating well, I had to work past the old habits and lies that I told myself.

The hard part was putting myself first, even above my own children. I had to write things down and be honest with myself. I had to stop telling myself things were hopeless, that I wasn't worth it, and it wasn't going to work. The things we tell ourselves are things we start to believe. When we start believing them, it becomes our reality. We can make ourselves sick by holding on to old beliefs and traumas.

I had to learn to love myself by setting healthy boundaries and working through my trauma. I learned which triggers have caused me to make bad decisions for myself. As I worked through this,

I learned to forgive myself and others and to let go of the pain I was holding. While I still deal with triggers, I have learned to identify and resolve them quickly so I can continue on with my day without having triggers set me back for days or even weeks like they did before.

In the beginning, I didn't know how to set healthy boundaries and I ran over people and pushed them away. I had no skills when it came to boundaries and I had no skills when it came to having any kind of healthy relationship.

I grew up with an alcoholic mother and abandonment issues, and I didn't learn how to function most of the time. What I considered common sense was completely different from other people's common sense. My first instinct was to manipulate, lie or avoid. I had a hard time learning how to be considerate, accountable and dependable.

I often felt out of place or stupid, and I rejected a lot of ideas because I was scared to admit that I didn't know how to do things because I was never taught them. I often faked my way through the world, or acted angry and abrasive so that people would keep their distance and not pressure me to do things that made me feel vulnerable.

As I learned to open up and be vulnerable, and as I learned skills to be reliable and trusting and open, I was able to be a little gentler on myself. Because of that, I was able to be a little gentler on others and my relationships. It changed the way I was as a mother and a friend.

All of these things helped me love myself, and set those healthy boundaries where I was able to put myself first without feeling so much guilt. I still struggle with it, but it's much easier than it was before. I can also enjoy the little things now and be in the present. I have learned to say no, and when I say yes I do so because I want to, not because I feel obligated to give my time. This shift in thinking and being has changed my life so I don't carry the resentment that I once did.

Our people carry so much resentment in so many ways. So much has been done through residential schools and child apprehension that it has taught us to believe we are ugly, dirty, stupid, and less than. We are not wanted, we are not important, we are worthless. We have been told we do not belong and are not human.

Many of these beliefs have been passed down to us through each generation, and it has become so normalized that we don't even realize we are thinking this way. It comes out in how we treat ourselves and how we treat our family, our community and our land.

My tema always used to tell me to pay attention to how I sat in a chair. She told me to never slouch at a meeting and that I should always listen. She told me to watch what I was thinking because the Creator could hear my thoughts, and the bad ones would make me sick. She told me to watch what I said because our words are powerful.

Our words and mind can make our bodies sick.

The things we hold on to and the things we tell ourselves stay in our body and manifest themselves as disease. I have seen it happen to many people in my own family and community, and in others through my travels across Canada.

I believe that as our people continue to call their spirits back and see the beauty in themselves, the sickness we see in our communities will start to disappear.

11

Residential school taught many of our people that we were inferior. It taught us how to obey and listen. It taught us that we were worthless and no one wanted us and that everything about us was wrong.

I was born to residential school survivors, but I didn't really know until I was older and my mom told me stories of being in residential school in Cranbrook. It wasn't until I was in my thirties that I learned my dad went to the Kamloops Residential School.

As I got older and really focused on my sobriety and wellness, I was drawn to work where I could sit in circles with groups of people who would end up sharing their life stories with me.

In the beginning, I sat with youth in foster care and youth who were transitioning out of it. They told me their stories about growing up in care, and their struggles and hurts. Sometimes I would leave those meetings and cry for an hour. Many of the youth I worked with have stayed connected to me and I have watched them grow over the years. I feel pride for what they have been able to accomplish for themselves.

In some of the sessions, our elders would share stories with the youth about their lives. Sometimes they would mention residential school and talk about what happened to them and how they were after they got out. They would share stories about starting their own families and how they didn't know how to be parents.

It was during those times I witnessed healing. I wasn't sure what it was at the time, but I knew the simple act of sharing out loud with one another helps people connect, and I knew that the connection between elders and youth was a sacred one.

My work with youth in care introduced me to many organizations who worked in trauma. One day I was asked to be a youth representative on a committee that advised the upcoming work with the Truth and Reconciliation Commission.[1] I started to hear more in-depth stories from our elders about what happened in residential school.

My parents and grandparents were sent to a place where the first thing they were forced to do was cut their hair. I was always told our hair is sacred and holds much of our power. Our hair can be used to hold prayers, and I was told if we didn't take care of our hair we could get sick.

When I brushed my hair, I wasn't allowed to just throw the loose strands in the garbage, and I was told never to flush it down the toilet. I had to take my hair outside and let it go in the wind, or burn it, and if there wasn't a safe place to take care of my hair I had to put it in my pocket until I could.

My mom told me to be very careful to never let anyone get hold of my hair, because the person who did could do love medicine with it and make me fall in love and I could get stuck with them forever.

My parents and grandparents were told not to speak their language in residential school. They were whipped and beaten. I heard stories of children having their tongues burned with needles. Some children had boiling water poured over their heads to rid these "dirty Indians" of lice. Sometimes the water was so scalding that the children would soil themselves and were beaten again for being dirty Indians who didn't know how to use the bathroom properly.

---

[1]   For more information on the Truth and Reconciliation Commission of Canada, go to www.trc.ca.

Our language proves how long we've been here and the strength of our understanding about the world around us: the connections, the land, the stars, and the things we can and cannot see.

My mom told me there is no way to lie in our language because it is so descriptive. She told me I needed to learn the language and know the stories of our waters and mountains and land.

There was language we learned as children, a baby language. Our people also have a high language which elders speak when it came to providing governance to our people. Our high language holds the way we make decisions and how we bring people together. There are very few people who remember it because of residential schools, and there are a lot of arguments today about some words that people don't remember, and words that some people think others are making up. These arguments happen between our people and divide our families, communities and nation. It is a direct result of the residential schools.

Everything we are lives in our language.

When our language was taken away in the residential schools, our people lost the connection to who we were. When our children went back home to their parents, they couldn't understand their language, and their parents didn't understand English.

Alcohol was introduced. Indians weren't allowed to leave the reserve or drink alcohol, but Indian agents would bring alcohol onto the reserve and give it to the people. Our people found that alcohol was a good way to hide the pain from losing their children.

When our children were taken away, it took away their parents' ability to parent. They forgot their roles as parents, and children were brought up by strangers who hurt and starved them.

Many times, I heard survivors say they waited for their parents and wondered why they didn't come. Many children didn't know what happened to them. Some children were allowed to come home for breaks while others didn't go home for eight years or more.

Some children said they came home to see parents they didn't recognize anymore. Their parents used to be loving people who spent time with them fishing or hunting or picking berries, but now they were people who were drinking and fighting. They were violent with each other.

These young people who came home ended up figuring things out on their own and found ways to survive. Some started to drink so they could forget what happened to them in residential school.

Many tried to start families of their own but had no healthy foundations for parenting. All they knew was the degradation they learned in residential schools. As a result, the government stole their babies from them.

Those children were taken away by the government and put into foster care, all because they believed mothers didn't know how to be mothers and fathers didn't know how to be fathers. And again, our children were raised without the language to connect them to who they were.

Those children became my parents, they became my husband Rob's parents, and as hard as our parents tried to make things better for us, we still felt the effects of what the residential schools did to our families.

When I was little, my teachers were the elders and ceremony people. They were very strict with their teachings and we had to listen to everything they told us. We weren't allowed to write anything down and we had to pay attention when they spoke.

Sometimes my mom would host teachers, ceremony people, singers and dancers in our home. Our house would be filled with people and we all had roles. My sister and I would sleep with my mom and give up our rooms to our guests, and we would wake up early before everyone else and start making breakfast for them.

Before ceremony, we would sit together and prepare medicine or cook things. We were told ceremony didn't start with sitting in a room with medicine and pipes and bundles, it started from the moment you woke up and continued in how you carried yourself through the day.

We had to be mindful of how we prepared things for ourselves and others, like beading or sewing, putting together bundles or cooking food. My mom told us we had to pray or meditate and think good thoughts while we did those things. She told us if we were grumpy or in a bad mood, we had to step away from what we were doing until we could gain control of our mind.

There were times when we had guests who would sit up with us all night and share their teachings. My mom would tell us she was determined to break the cycle of dysfunction, and the only way she knew how was to teach us to be proud of who we were and to be proud to be Native.

Back then I rarely saw women with medicine, but I knew we had them in our nation. They were the ones who had the winter lodges or longhouses to host winter dances. They were also called winter hops, and my mom would bring us when we were little. They would always start with a dinner and then close the door when the ceremony started, and we would sing and dance past midnight. There were many reasons for the winter dance for the Syilx people, and it was necessary to get our people prepared for the coming year.

One night we sat up until the sun came up with a visitor from Saskatchewan. I was very tired, but I stayed awake because this teacher was telling us prophecies. He told us he was only allowed to share them at certain times of the year and day.

It was the late '80s and I was eleven years old. It was at a time when I didn't see a lot of people with medicine, and when I did they were usually called medicine men. Many of these medicine men didn't call themselves medicine men, they called themselves helpers.

One of the things he told us was that our people were starting on this journey and they would begin to heal. He told us that they were too scared to hold their own medicine, and so they would call on medicine people to come pray for them or with them because they didn't know how to pray.

Everyone has the ability to hold their own medicine, and one day we will start to see people gathering medicines and having their own medicine bundles. We will see that our people who hold medicine will be younger and younger.

People often thought the prayers of this man were more powerful than others because he had a medicine bundle, but it wasn't true. He told us that our own prayers and voices are the most powerful, because only we know what we truly want.

As I got older, I started to meet more women who held medicine and pipes and bundles, and I was told how to carry myself. I was told to pay attention to the way I walked in the world and to respect myself and the men in my life. I was told to never step over their legs or share the same bed with them when I was on my moon time. There was a balance that needed to be maintained, and women had to be strong and disciplined because we are the backbone of our people.

When I think of all of the teachings I have received, I think about growing up as a woman with these teachings and how I actually applied them. I realize I wasn't always successful because of all the underlying anger I had toward men.

Sometimes I would make myself feel superior to men because I was a woman, but I really didn't feel strong. I also felt anger and disdain toward women, because I thought most were disrespectful and weak.

My mom had her stroke when I was nineteen, a time I was becoming an adult. I stumbled through my twenties trying to piece together who I was and looked for women I could learn from.

I never learned how to be a woman in this world because I didn't know what it meant to be one. What I learned were things I was supposed to do and how I was supposed to carry myself, but no one taught me how to do that and trudge through my trauma at the same time.

12

I feel blessed by the people my mom surrounded me with while I was growing up. Not only did she start taking me to powwows and ceremony when she got sober, but she also started taking me to meetings.

They weren't just any meetings. They were political meetings talking about land issues and our nation. I sat in band and nation meetings with provincial and federal governments who were present to talk about what it was we were so mad about.

As young as I was, even I knew the people sitting across the table had absolutely no respect for our leadership, and it was the first time I really had a surge of pride about who I was and where I came from, because our leadership didn't back down to anyone.

At the time, we had elders who spoke our language and told the stories of our land and our responsibilities. We had academics and knowledge keepers who translated and explained our responsibilities and our inherent rights to people who had absolutely no understanding of these concepts. We had hardcore militants in army fatigues who let them know we weren't afraid to fight for our land, and we had leaders who had been a part of the American Indian Movement and the Red Power movement, and many who had travelled across North America with my dad.

In 1990, communities across Canada started to pay attention to the Mohawk warriors and their fight to stop a development that would desecrate their sacred burial grounds with a golf course. It turned into an armed standoff known as the 1990 Oka Crisis. The situation became escalated and tensions rose as the army was called in to "handle" the situation.

The Penticton Indian Band set up its own blockade that stood for eighty-seven days in support of Oka and the Mohawk people. The Okanagan people came together and organized a peace run from the Okanagan territory to Oka. It was a time when our people started to stand up, and I remember hearing my mom say over and over again that it was time our voices were heard and that we would no longer be a passive people to the government.

I attended meetings in the nation as a youth representative, sitting at the table and listening to some of our most inspirational and recognized leaders stand up to government.

My mom was really good friends with one of our council members, Stewart Phillip, and his wife Joan. He would eventually become chief of the Penticton Indian Band, grand chief and chair of the Okanagan Nation Alliance, and president of the Union of B.C. Indian Chiefs. Today he is known across the country as Dr. Grand Chief Stewart Phillip, a lifelong advocate for human rights and land.

My mom would sit for hours with Joan and they would go back and forth laughing and joking and sharing stories about their families and their sobriety. Then they would go on to more serious issues and the politics our people were facing.

My mom and I would ride with them to meetings. I sat in the back of the car and listened to the adults talk about who they thought would attend, and they would predict what was going to happen. After the meeting they talked about the things that transpired and what the next steps would be. Almost always, we would stop at a Chinese restaurant to have the all-you-can-eat smorgasbord.

I would get so passionate about what was being said that my body would get tense. That's when I realized I had something in my blood that made me want to fight for our people. I sat on the

Oka blockade for the majority of the time and spent thirty-six hours awake with two of my friends while we shared stories until we didn't make any sense to each other anymore.

Racial tension kept getting worse. It got to the point where our teachers began making remarks during classes and our parents decided to pull us all out of school. They opened up our community hall and brought in books for us to read. Our parents volunteered to teach us and eventually signed us up for long-distance classes until they figured out a way to get our own school established.

My mom sat me down and asked me what I wanted to do. She had two schools in mind, but it would be up to me whether I wanted to go. We decided to check out both schools. One was in Northern Manitoba at a place called the Turtle Lodge that housed a very well-respected traditional man. He travelled the world and spoke about prophecies, Indigenous cultures and preserving our traditional ways. It was an amazing experience to be there, but at the time I didn't realize what an honour it was to meet him and his family.

Then we went to Alberta, where a school was structured around academics but also incorporated the Blackfeet language. I decided I didn't want to fall too far behind in my academics because I wanted to get into political science and maybe become the first woman to sit as national chief for the Assembly of First Nations, or even prime minister. I wanted to be a writer, a lawyer, or something or someone who made a difference.

I spent a lot of time with leadership. I would take notes and go with my mom when she would visit them. When I was small, my tema was the one who would take me to the elders' meetings where they talked about a number of things concerning our community, our families and how things should be done.

My family was very particular in how they participated in our community. Despite all the things my mom went through and how she parented in her alcoholism, she was still well loved and respected in our community.

Growing up I realized so many of our people went through the same things and learned the same hurts as I did. I learned that we were all just doing the best we could.

My tupa, my grandfather, was chief of our community for over twenty years and I grew up learning what a great and well-respected man he was. Many people told me he was the best chief ever. Even though he died before I was born, my mom always talked about him and community members always shared with me what they remembered of him.

My tupa was a listener. He would visit everyone at their homes and ask them what their thoughts were. My sister's godmother told me we didn't have a band office back in the day, so when people wanted to talk to the chief they would just go to his house and my tema would open the door and make something to eat and drink for the visitor. My tupa would sit with them and listen to what they had to say, and then try to find a way to help or make it right.

My uncles who helped raise my little sister and me would always share our tupa's teachings with us about how we were supposed to listen, behave and act. My mom shared teachings on how we had to listen to everyone because everyone was important, and even if we didn't like them we still had something to learn from them.

It became my practice to listen to people and try to figure out where they were coming from. As I got older, I stopped trying to figure them out and started listening. The skills I learned as a child and a youth listening to and learning from my community members became my greatest strength.

I became someone who could listen and then share the stories back in great detail. To this day I am able to recall things said a long time ago. Sometimes I won't even remember until the moment I share them.

I was little during a time when our elders still mentored young people. I can look around my community at the families and see the knowledge passed down to them and the contributions they make to take care of our communities and the land. I know there is no right or wrong way to do it, because without each of us contributing in the ways we know how, things would be forgotten.

13

I dropped out of school in Grade 9 because I could not get past math, and the experience left me feeling stupid in all areas of my life. School left me with a beaten self-esteem and sense of worthlessness.

I managed to pass Grade 10 and 11 classes through distance learning. The only way I got through math was because one of my instructors saw my potential. She knew I was struggling but had tried different ways to learn, so she gave me the questions to my big test and I memorized all the answers.

I was nineteen years old when I moved to the United States and took an entrance test for mature students at a local university. I passed everything except for math, but the university accepted me as a mature student anyway and put me in the most basic math class they had, but I still couldn't get it. I worked part time as a bartender at night and went to school during the day, but I only made it through two semesters before I dropped out after taking all the English courses I could.

When I moved back to Canada and tried to enrol at Okanagan College, they told me my credits wouldn't transfer from the States and I would have to start all over again. I decided to give up on school at that point, because it didn't feel worth it anymore.

As I ended my "youth years," as defined by provincial standards, an opportunity came up to apply for an Aboriginal youth internship program with the provincial government. The position offered nine months working for a government ministry and three months with an Aboriginal organization.

I applied because I didn't need to have my Grade 12, since the age range for the positions was eighteen to twenty-nine years old. I secured a position with the Ministry of Children and Family Development and found ways to get experience and mentorship in policy, and I learned about legislation and the United Nations Declaration of the Rights of the Child. When I completed my one-year internship, the Ministry of Children and Family Development offered me a full-time position with the interior region doing program and project development.

I wondered if they would realize how little education I had, and I waited for the moment when they would call me in and tell me I didn't qualify for the job. However, when I went in to sign all my papers they told me if I stayed on there was potential for me to further my education and work toward my Bachelor of Social Work.

I was six months into my full-time position with the province when I realized I couldn't do the work anymore. I couldn't work within a corporate system that seemed to care more about policies than people. When a job came up for a Comprehensive Community Plan coordinator (CCP coordinator) position, I felt that I had to apply for it.

I believe working for your own community can be one of the most rewarding and heartbreaking experiences of your life. Growing up in community means everyone knows what is happening in your life.

Community can be the safest place to be when the outside world is going crazy and it can also be the most grounding place to be when tragedy hits, because when it all comes down to it, we are all family.

When I first started as CCP coordinator, I sat in my office to create a work plan that I thought would be the best approach to creating a community plan. It wasn't long before our chief told me that it was the people who would tell me what the work plan would be.

He told me that in order to find out I should be visiting everyone and listening to what they wanted, instead of sitting at a desk trying to think of what they might want. He wanted to know not just what voting adults wanted, but what the kids, elders and different families wanted to see in their community plan.

Throughout the first year, Anona the communications coordinator and I spent much of our time doing home visits with elders, visiting schools and hosting lunches and dinners with anyone who would talk to us. It became clear in the first few months that there was absolutely no trust in our community. Many of them said there was no point in sharing anything with us because no one would listen anyway.

After a few meetings we would head back to our office and go through the notes, writing down things people had told us to do. They would tell us how we should conduct meetings and what we should talk about and who we should talk to. We made plans to do many of the things people told us to do.

It took a while, but eventually people started to realize we were listening to them, and more and more people started to attend meetings and contribute their thoughts. We started to host family meetings and pulled together everything we could into our plan.

The process took about four years to create a really good plan. It incorporated as many voices and perspectives as we could, even the things we didn't agree with.

There were times when it felt like we were constantly being attacked for not doing things the right way. Then there were moments where our community held us up for doing such good work. At times I felt like I was living in an abusive relationship.

There was a moment when I felt like the bad was overpowering the good, and I refused to attend band meetings because I felt like I was constantly being criticized by a specific group of people. They had gossiped about me and made comments about the way

I did things for the majority of my life. Whenever I had to deal with them, I always felt like a little girl again.

I went to visit our family friend and community leader Stewart Philip. He and Joan took me as their daughter, and I relied on their guidance for so many aspects of my life. He listened to my concerns about community planning, and finally said, "You know, you want to get to this place of euphoria where everyone gets along and everything is perfect. You just want to be parachuted right down into the middle of it. That's not how life works. You have to go through it in order to get to the middle. That's how you grow. You have to do the things you don't always want to do. You know, if by chance someone decided to give us a billion dollars one day, it wouldn't fix anything. Things would go along for a little bit, but then the same old issues would start to pop up again. You can't hide from it. You cannot tiptoe around the edges; you have to go through it." He then shared with me about a time when he got really sick.

"When I was really sick, I was close to the end. Cancer, you know. I lost a bunch of weight and it wasn't looking good. I was afraid to fall asleep, so I would stay up all night until the sun came up and then I'd go to bed. But as I would walk around in the living room looking out the windows, I would look at the cherry trees in our backyard and think, If I can just make it to see the cherry tree blossom, then I know I'll be okay.

"And I made it. It was a miracle and I remember going back to my very first community meeting as chief after almost dying from cancer. A community member stood up and just gave it to me. He yelled at me the whole time and I just sat there and took it and inside I was smiling because I was just so happy to be there and be alive."

He shared many things with me, and after he finished I would sit there in silence, and we would look around the room before he would start sharing updates with me on other political matters, or he would ask me how my mom and sister were doing and how the kids were. We would visit until it was time to go or one of his grandchildren called him.

So many of the decisions I make and the work I do in politics has been greatly influenced by his leadership and courage. He has always reflected on stories from the past, and there is always a beginning to these stories. They go back to time immemorial.

He shared his story with me about being apprehended as a baby and being taken into foster care and being alone. He also talked about his return to the community after his father had found him.

He told me he was visiting his father once and looking out the window, and he started to question things, like why his fields were dry. His father explained the situation to him, about how our water was rerouted to settlers for their orchards and cattle. He felt an intense sense of injustice that caused him to ask more questions and learn. He eventually became involved in the Red Power movement that brought him and Joan together.

Joan's ex-husband was Joe Face, my late stepfather who tragically passed away during our family trip to Vancouver Island. Their son Monty would become one of the most important people in my life. They had other sons who became like brothers to me, and we have shared many stories over the years.

Joan and Stewart always told me that whatever work they don't accomplish in their lifetime will be left for their children. They have inspired many and have been called on to support communities across our country. Many leaders have held them up for their support and the comfort they bring to communities who face immense oppression by outside governments.

They told me love is always the answer. Love people where they are and always listen and pay attention. When I would write, Stewart would tell me to copyright it. But when I would speak he told me to never write things down and speak from the heart.

After speaking with Stewart and Joan, I would go home and think about it for a day or two before gathering up my courage to continue the work that needed to be done. As I listened to those stories and watched him in his work, I always hoped that I could have the courage and control over myself like he did. He was an expert at listening and watching for things other people didn't notice. He always listened to people with love in his heart, even when they were ripping him apart.

I continued to visit with other people in our community who would share advice on how to advance the community plan, and we were able to move our community forward because we took the time to make those visits, not just to share our success but also to honestly share our challenges with them.

We learned that the very act of listening and taking the time to gather the different voices and perspectives of people would provide us with an opportunity to heal together. We provided spaces where we would commit to hearing and listening to what each other was saying instead of always trying to tear each other down.

We set goals on how we would gather and meet, and what our expectations were of each other. It worked at the time and people started implementing action items on their own, in their own families, and they were also building the community members' ideas into their own work plans.

Based on our Four Food Chiefs story, our community plan and process became so successful that we were highlighted at provincial and national meetings. We continued to step outside of the prescriptive ways professional planners used and stopped trying to predict what was going to happen. We were able to do so much more within our own community when we relied on our own people instead of utilizing outside consultants to do the work for us.

As my contract with my community as a CCP coordinator was coming to an end, I was called away to do so many workshops and keynotes across the province that I ended up starting my own consulting company so that I could do the work in my own name.

Many people called me crazy, because I left a job with benefits to start my own company when my daughter was just six months old. The first three years in business were scary; I was in the red and barely made it through. I had a lot of debt to pay off and I had no credit because of my previous lifestyle choices, including spending too much on drinking. I had no savings and had to figure out how to manage money as I went.

I went to visit my godparents, Adam and Sandi, who had been instrumental in my sobriety and recovery. They were both business owners and had years of sobriety and business experience. Whenever I was stuck in my professional and personal life, I knew I could visit them and ask for their advice on managing a business.

They shared their thoughts with me on how to be successful, but they also shared with me the emotions that come with becoming a business owner. They talked about the things that might hold me back and how scary it might be. They talked about what other people might say to make me question myself. They told me I was capable of doing it as long as I continued to make my sobriety number one. As our visit came to an end, my godfather told me that if an opportunity came up for me and I needed help to come and ask him.

It was his faith in me that helped me move forward, but I also knew the offer came with the condition that I had to be responsible and accountable, and by then there had been very few times in my life where I had actually followed through.

I knew when the time came to ask for help it would be more than just swallowing my pride. It would be dealing with my inner voice that told me I didn't need anyone's help, and if I asked for help I was weak.

I knew I would need to be responsible and set real goals for myself so that I didn't let him down. But, more importantly, I couldn't let myself down.

14

Having my own company put me into a lot of spaces dominated by men. At almost every table, and because I had a hard time feeling safe in those spaces, I put up walls and my behaviour reflected my fear.

I had to learn how to get my message across so I felt heard, and most times no one would listen to me unless I sold my idea to a male colleague who shared my idea. I had to stay quiet at times I knew I should say something, and I had to put up with comments from people who didn't find anything wrong with the negative way they addressed me or talked about others.

I worked in both the political realm and the business realm and I felt fairly confident in both spaces, but I still felt like I was playing a role. I had to dress and act a certain way, and always felt like I had to have an air of self-importance and coldness to make sure people didn't get too close to me.

I was in my late thirties when I started to feel like I was in a position to say no to opportunities and not worry about whether another opportunity would come up. I was also of the mentality that the only way I would be successful was if I hustled and worked long hours. I took pride in my work ethic and worked eighteen-hour days, slept four, and spent time in the gym for the other two hours.

My presence at home and time with Phoenix suffered, but I thought I was making a better life for her because she was able to do things that I never did as a child. I was busy working contracts:

I took a job with the federal government in the Community Initiatives Unit, I was helping with the CCP Mentorship Initiative in B.C., and I was putting forward recommendations to take the Mentorship Initiative national.

I was heavily involved in advising businessmen who were in partnerships with Indigenous communities. I helped companies who were interested in joint ventures with communities, specifically with cannabis companies who were preparing for legalization in Canada.

I was also helping with an upcoming provincial gathering of federal representatives and Indigenous leadership in B.C. It was an annual event called the Joint Gathering, which showcased some of the best practices in the province, upcoming issues and legislation, and other key initiatives.

That year I would also present at one of the main plenaries, which meant I would be speaking in front of all the leadership present. It was one of the first big highlights of my professional career, and I was extremely proud of myself for the way I presented and spoke to the room.

When I was done my presentation I went outside of the ballroom, as I needed to get ready to attend a meeting at another hotel with an investor and some impressive businessmen. I had connected with this group earlier that year and was excited about this opportunity.

On my way I was stopped by a young man who wanted my contact information. He wanted me to work with his community, so I put my phone down on a nearby table and stopped to write down my email address for him, because I had left my business cards in my purse with my jacket back in the ballroom. Just as I was standing back up from leaning over the table to write, someone came up behind me and put their hand on my waist just above my rear end.

The touch shocked me, and the young man I was talking to looked uncomfortable and quickly excused himself. I turned to see one of our long-standing chiefs and prominent leaders standing there, waiting to give me a hug.

I quickly shook off the violated feeling I had as a mistake and gave him a hug. He told me he was proud of the impressive work I was doing and wanted me to know I had done a good job. I was flattered and still a little shaken, but I thanked him and let him know I had to get to another meeting. I ran to the bathroom before leaving the building.

Once I was done in the bathroom, I raced for the elevator to catch it before it closed, and a briefcase came up to catch the doors. It was the same leader and chief I had just finished talking with by the table. He smiled and said, "I would stop the world for you" as I stepped into the elevator.

The comment made me a little uncomfortable, but I laughed it off as the doors closed. There was a hotel employee in the elevator with us, but the employee got off when the elevator stopped on the next floor.

As soon as the elevator doors closed, this older gentleman—a chief, a leader, an international advocate, a father, and a husband—decided to come across the elevator, pull me into a tight embrace and put his hands where they shouldn't have been and put his face into my neck, making a sound that made me push myself back.

Immediately, we were both embarrassed and I started to make silly small talk. I said, "So where are you going? Oh yeah, I'm going to a meeting . . . yep, that's nice. Oh, wow."

As soon as the elevator doors opened I bolted to the left and raced out the building and down the street without my jacket, and realized that I had left my phone on the table back in the hotel. I decided to leave it in hopes I could go back and retrieve it from the registration desk later.

As soon as I got to my next meeting, I sat down completely distracted and couldn't concentrate. My friend and colleague put her hand on my bare shoulder and I jumped as she asked me if I was cold. I told her I was fine and had left my jacket at the other hotel. Our meeting didn't last long, so I had to walk in the cold to my hotel, where I had a message waiting for me that my manager had my phone at the office.

I had dinner plans with a friend, but I was still distracted and not feeling well about what had happened, so I mentioned it casually as we were having dinner. I told him something weird had happened and I didn't know what to think about it. He looked a little upset and said very simply, "That's sexual assault."

It took me a minute to think about it because I immediately denied it. For me, sexual assault was when someone attacked and raped you. I kept thinking that there was some other reason I felt the way I did, but I didn't want to admit that what had happened to me was sexual assault because I didn't do or say anything to respond or address it when it happened.

My friend asked me what I was going to do about it, and I said I didn't know. He told me that I should go to our mutual mentor and talk to him about it, and I agreed that I would when I got home the next day.

I woke up with a feeling of fear. I didn't know where it was coming from. The name of the person who had grabbed me in the elevator popped into my head and I started fearing I would have to see him.

I packed up my things and headed back to Penticton, where I spent some time at home. I still didn't feel good, but I was happy to be home with my kids. We went out to eat like we usually did when I got home, and when we got back to our house I went straight to my room and watched TV until I fell asleep.

The next morning, I woke up again with a sinking feeling in my stomach. I didn't want to get out of bed, and I didn't want to deal with how I was feeling. I began to get angry, but I was too tired to even process it. I started to feel a little depressed and wondered if I was getting sick, but I knew I was just emotionally exhausted and figured I was just burning out. It took another day before I made myself go to my mentors' home to talk about what had happened to me, and to see if they felt I was making a big deal out of something that I shouldn't be dwelling on.

Their home was only a few houses down from mine, so it wasn't a big trip, but it felt really overwhelming. I drove by their house and continued to drive around for a bit before I finally decided to go back closer to the evening. When I got there, only Joan was home and I almost felt a sense of relief about it.

When I walked in she immediately offered me some tea, and we sat down at her kitchen table. I told her what had happened and she became visibly upset. We talked for a few more hours and she said that she would come with me to the police station to make a formal complaint, even though I knew that nothing would ever be done with it.

15

The next month or two was a struggle for me. I couldn't get out of bed and I wasn't eating. I woke up every day with an impending sense of doom. I would have fits of anger and break down easily. I felt like I was going crazy, and I was having a hard time dealing with what was happening to me.

I would go to the gym and listen to music and work out really hard. I would feel the anger coming, and before I knew it I had tears running down my face and I wasn't sure why.

I was scared to be around Phoenix. Her dad was now in a relationship and making trips out of the province to see his girlfriend, so I was left alone with her and felt trapped when I couldn't run.

There was one day in particular that I just couldn't deal with my emotions, and I felt like I was going to burst. I was having thoughts of hurting myself, of hitting things and wanting to run, maybe even to drink, and I felt stuck because Phoenix was with me. I was furious because her dad was gone, and I felt he should have known that I wasn't in a good state of mind and we needed him around. I called him and yelled at him while Phoenix followed me around the house. I was trying to get away to have some privacy to tell him what was going on with me. I just couldn't stop crying, and he told me to get to a meeting.

At the time, my Kyle was still living with me but was spending time with his girlfriend and friends, so I asked him if he could watch his sister so that I could attend a meeting.

I had rebelled against these AA meetings for the majority of my life for a number of reasons. My mom used to take me when I would try to stop drinking, but I would go, listen, leave and not return. I really didn't understand AA meetings at the time; they didn't make sense to me and I just wasn't ready to admit that I needed any kind of help.

After I started to appreciate their value, I personally found that these meetings were a safe space for me to go and listen to other people who have the same crazy thinking patterns as I do, and who are dealing with the same issues and challenges. Everyone in the room wants the same thing: sobriety.

The first few times I quit drinking, I was full of myself and really felt like I was above others, but those small stints of sobriety never lasted. I learned that my drinking had nothing to do with alcohol and everything to do with a refusal to deal with my pain and feelings.

It was humbling to realize that I was the only one responsible for my life, and no one was going to help me, save me, or fix me but myself. There were many different steps and readings that helped me figure out how to function in a world where everyone else seemed to know the rules but me.

After the incident in the elevator, I went to a meeting and was asked to share. I broke down and shared everything that had happened to me the month prior, and I talked about how scared I was. I felt like my feelings and my body didn't belong to me anymore and I didn't know what was wrong with me. I was worried I was broken and was going to go crazy, and I thought I was going to have to see a doctor about my mental health and be committed to an institution.

I shared my story openly, and by the end of the meeting I had received so much love and words of wisdom that I felt a little safer in the world. One of the women I knew came up to me and asked if she could visit me afterwards and said she would bring potato chips.

I laughed and made myself say yes. Deep down I didn't want company, because I was so used to being in my own space and dealing with my own things that it was really hard for me to open up my personal space to others. However, in my heart I knew it was important for me to take this offer.

She came up to see me later that evening and we sat on the couch in my living room while I cried and shared some more, and she shared a few stories of her own. She explained to me that she had gone through something called post-traumatic stress disorder, or complex traumatic stress. She explained what happened to her and how she dealt with it, and many things started to make sense to me. I started to feel a little less crazy.

Before she left, she said she wanted to share a story with me. As she began, I realized that she was telling me the story my tema would tell me at bedtime and I started to cry. I felt my tema there in the room and knew that I was going to be okay.

After she finished the story, she told me the Creator doesn't just make us strong. The Creator doesn't just pour strong into the top of your head and then *bam*, you're strong! The Creator gives us these challenges in life, and we have to work through them in order to prepare us for the work ahead of us that requires this strength.

We hugged and she left. That moment and visit changed my life and how I was going to deal with things moving forward.

16

The next day I started to look for a trauma therapist, and I made a commitment I would attend two to three meetings a week to keep me on track and feeling supported.

The previous month or so I had felt completely alone and isolated, and I pushed people away in anger. I felt like no one knew what I was going through and I really didn't know how to explain it anyway. It was like I was drowning, and when people tried to help me I refused to grab their hand.

I had written an open letter in the first few days after the incident had happened. At first it was just for me to get out all of my feelings, and then I decided I wanted to send it to the chief who had accosted me, but I wasn't sure where to send it. I didn't want to send it to his office, because I knew the receptionist sometimes opened letters and recorded them.

I didn't want to send it to his home, because I knew his wife might find it. I wasn't sure why I wanted to send it to him, but I felt like he needed to know that what he had done was not right or appropriate, and I felt like he needed to know how it had affected me.

At the time I was still working in a position with the federal government, and I hadn't gone back to Vancouver to my office as I was working remotely. I was having a hard time writing and concentrating and felt like I had a bad case of writer's block.

I felt like my employer at the time needed to know what was going on with me, so I wrote them an email explaining what I had been working through.

It wasn't long before they reached out to me and invited me to come in to talk to someone, while also offering me a 1-800 number for emergency counselling.

I agreed to come in and meet with them to find out what their purpose was for wanting to meet with me. I walked into the office and there were three people sitting there. One was my manager and the other two were from other departments, there to share supports and options so I could try to deal with what had happened to me.

They let me know I could make a police report, make a formal complaint and take it through the legal process, and that I could do mediation.

They told me I had some time to think about it and gave me the name and number of people I could connect with. They also let me know I would have my counselling sessions covered through my work.

I walked out of the office and wandered around downtown Vancouver for a while, thinking about what I wanted to do or if I should do anything at all. As I was walking past the stores, I saw a really nice dress in the window and then thought I shouldn't even look at it because it just called for unwanted attention. The moment the thought crossed my mind, I caught it and became angry.

I started to think about the way my life had started to change because of what had happened. I had started changing the way I dressed, because on the day I was touched and grabbed I was wearing a tight black dress and I thought I probably shouldn't have worn it.

I knew that those thoughts were the result of what had happened to me, and it drove me to want to move forward and do something, but I really didn't know what to do. I had known this man most of my adult life, and I saw him as a role model and a leader, as someone who was held up by many people. At the same time, some people were afraid and intimidated by his presence. He also had a lot of experience with politics and legal action, and he had powerful connections. I felt that if I tried to do anything to discredit him, my voice would be completely disregarded and cast aside.

I also thought about his family, his wife, and his grown children. When you grow up in politics or business or entertainment in the Indigenous community, you end up crossing paths with the same people over and over again and everyone knows everyone. I didn't want to cause problems.

I thought about all the things that made him a good man and a good leader. I had felt inspired by him on so many occasions and felt so much pride when I heard him speak. To me he was closer to an elder, because there had been times when he had shared his advice and thoughts with me.

I worried about my professional career. I was just getting started as a consultant, and I felt like if said anything it would follow me. I didn't think people would want to work with me if I complained about sexual harassment or assault. I worried people might think I was a troublemaker and wouldn't want to work with me in case I accused them of being inappropriate as well.

I was upset because, while I had heard about this individual's reputation for inappropriate advances on young women growing up and throughout my life, I always felt safe and protected because of who my mentors were, as if their reputations alone would protect me from advances like this. I also felt like I should be immune from these kinds of incidents because I never put myself in positions that might bring me trouble. I never attended receptions or galas where they were serving alcohol, with the exception of two gatherings later on in my life where I was asked to attend because of the position I was in at the time.

My mind went through so many stages: anger, fear, hopelessness, instability, and confusion. At times I was totally irrational. I tried to manage all the feelings that came up as I struggled with post-traumatic stress. Looking back, I can understand why so many women may not come forward after a sexual assault. If it was anything like my experience, they fear being labelled crazy and difficult as they constantly wonder if what happened *had* really happened, and if it was a big deal or not.

I was upset because I wanted to be protected. I wanted someone to say something on my behalf to stop his behaviour. I was upset because no one had stopped him before. I thought about all the leaders and male colleagues I had worked with in the past who had gotten away with such bad behaviour, and I became upset at all the women who didn't speak up about this before it had affected me personally.

Until this point I had gone through life working and hustling with people who were older and more experienced than me, and so I accepted everything as "just the way it is." I didn't question anyone, and I just did the work I was supposed to do and always felt a sense of accomplishment when I was praised for it.

I put my feelings aside, I put my complaints aside, and I put a piece of myself aside every time I had to occupy different spaces. At the time, I didn't know what patriarchy meant. I had heard people mention it and talk about it, but I never really understood what it meant and the role it played in my life.

It wasn't until I was stuck dealing with my emotions, questioning why people were allowed to behave this way and why no one did anything, that I really started to understand what patriarchy was all about. Until that point I even had a hard time understanding what "old boys' club" meant—I thought it just meant a club of old guys.

Through my life I had been in constant survival mode, just trying to function by focusing on making sure I was able to pay my bills and feed my kids. There was very little I knew about underlying issues and root causes about why things were the way they were.

It wasn't until I went through this breaking point that I really started to learn what my responsibility was as a woman, and what it meant to be a woman. I had spent most of my time growing up trying not to be a woman, because I thought women were weak and got hurt.

17

While I had been thinking a lot about the situation, I was still confused about how I should move forward. The third party connected to my employer kept calling me from Ottawa wanting to know my decision. They left messages and emailed asking for an answer, and I just kept ignoring the calls because I didn't know yet. I became upset a few times and felt like they weren't helping me, just making it worse.

It wasn't until I was able to sit at the water and talk to my family and friends that I was able to gather the courage I needed to ask for a mediation. My godmother Sandi talked to me again about all the feelings I would go through, and she told me there would be moments when I would have doubt.

She told me I was allowed to be a beautiful woman and wear beautiful dresses, and I was even allowed to feel sexy and good in my skin. She told me the following few months were going to be hard and I would feel fear, but I would have to go through it and do it anyway if I wanted to get past all this.

I was preparing to go through a formal process and wanted to have a mediation. I thought really hard about what I wanted it to look like.

At first I thought I wanted to host a circle and invite witnesses and people who gave me strength to be there. I thought of asking my support system and even my son to let this man know what his actions did to me and my family. I thought of asking for men only and then women only, and then a combination of all before I finally decided I needed to do it by myself.

I decided I needed to do it alone for many reasons, and even though it terrified me I knew I had to do it, even when I thought I might not be able to.

One thing stood out in my mind that helped me move forward. It was when Joan told me, "After you do this, no one will ever touch you again." I don't know how many times I broke down and cried when I thought of her saying those words to me.

Among the many reasons that moved me toward this decision, the biggest driver for me was knowing that what had happened to me made me come very close to losing my sobriety, my health, my well-being, and my livelihood.

I was in my mid-thirties. I had a fair amount of experience. I had grown up in this world. I was connected to influential people. I had a number of years of sobriety under me and had done some intense healing work. I had a support system of people who were not afraid to tell me what I needed, and I knew that I wasn't alone. And yet I still hit the ground and almost gave up. I still thought of self-harm and felt like I was on the verge of insanity. Even though I had gone through a complete and total breakdown, I was totally supported by people who helped me come back from it.

I thought of all of this and then I thought of younger women. I thought of women who wanted to make a difference and work for their people, but who might not have the same experience or support as me. I thought of them and how I would feel if this happened to them and I hadn't said anything. I knew I had to say something.

I decided that I would deal with everything as it came. I thought of all the things that could happen to me, and I realized I could do anything with my life. I didn't have to be a consultant. I could get a job doing anything. I thought that if there were people who didn't want to work with me because I had spoken out about this person, then I probably didn't want to work with them anyway.

I went through my employer, who set me up with a mediator. The mediator contacted me and asked me when I was available to meet. It was then the end of January. The incident had happened in November.

The mediator let me know that the other party had also expressed their desire to get it over with as quickly as possible, but that he wasn't available to do this work until March.

I let them know that it was fine with me, as I had a lot of work and preparation to do. It also felt like a long way away and I knew that having that much time to think also left me the opportunity to back out. I decided that I would stay committed and continue to remind myself of what I had just gone through. I had to remind myself that what I experienced was real and what I felt was valid.

I searched a lot of websites over the coming months looking up how to deal with sexual assault. This was before the #MeToo movement and it was around the same time the sexual assault story broke about Jian Ghomeshi.

I remember working out on the elliptical and watching the news as they were flashing statistics across the screen about how many women were assaulted per year, how many were actually reported, and how many were dismissed.

I continued to work with a therapist. I learned about what happened to my brain. I found out that when I was little all of these memories and traumas were stored in a box in my brain. To protect me, my brain closed the lid and put away the box.

I always knew bad things had happened to me when I was little, but I never really recalled specifics.

My therapist told me that when I was put in that situation in the elevator, the experience tapped at the box that was in my brain and opened up the lid to traumas that happened to me as a child. He talked to me about why I was behaving the way I was, which was a normal response to being triggered by a traumatic memory.

I felt I understood what was going on in my brain. I was able to deal with it and work through it. I didn't feel like I was going crazy anymore.

As the mediation date got closer, I increased my attendance at meetings. I spoke about what was happening to me out loud with others at meetings and connected with people who went through the same thing as I did. I also started praying every day for myself, my brain, my heart and my courage. I prayed for my children and hoped that what I was going through wasn't affecting them.

A couple of weeks before the mediation meeting, the mediator called me to give me the location. I felt myself get cold as he told me it was the same hotel where the incident had occurred. He quickly apologized and offered to change the location.

I told him it wasn't necessary; I believed everything was meant to be the way it was and felt it was a good opportunity for me to move past anything that might hold me back from moving forward.

The day before the mediation, I travelled to Vancouver by myself. I floated around the city and tried to prepare myself for the next day. I had dinner with one of my friends and colleagues named Sandra whom I had worked with on many projects over the years. She asked me how I was feeling and listened as I told her what I was going through. She helped affirm my experience, and she and her partner walked me back to my room after dinner.

That night I couldn't stop crying and didn't know if I was going to be able to do it. I decided to open up my Facebook, and as I surfed through my friends' newsfeeds I decided I would share what I was going through in the most vulnerable way possible:

> I think for the most part the people on my friends
> list love me. You might not like me all the time.
> But I know you probably love me. I'm asking for
> prayers for tomorrow morning [March 27, 2015].

4 months ago in November 2014, I was inappropriately groped in an elevator by someone in a position of power. For the last 4 months it has affected me mentally, emotionally, spiritually and physically. I decided to take a stand and for the first bit I struggled on my own with what happened. I was full of fear and anger and rage and blame and shame and self-pity. It took me a moment to pull myself together. I knew that I wasn't the only one this happened to. But I ignored it because it didn't happen to me. I thought I was safe because of the way I carried myself . . . I was angry because it happened. I was angry at the women before me who never said anything and angry at his peers for knowing his behaviour and not saying anything. I didn't want to say anything to cause problems, to create drama. I didn't want people to think I was a troublemaker or unprofessional. I have struggled with what people would think. About being discredited for making a big deal about nothing. Because everyone else brushes it aside as something some men just do. We normalize and allow it. But it's not in me to do that. My mom didn't always know how to stick up for me when I was younger but as I got older she did start sticking up for herself and showed me how to. I learned to not be quiet. I was a victim as a child and I didn't learn boundaries and even protected my abusers. We have to allow space for people to share and say no and set boundaries. We have to hold people accountable. We have to tell people that their actions that harm will no longer be tolerated no matter who they are. This is one of the most scary things I've ever

done, but one of the best things I have ever done for myself. I could take the easy way and let it slide and live my life, or I can take the not so easy way and grow from this. I am having a face to face with the person who was inappropriate with me tomorrow morning. I'm a little anxious, but I'll say my prayers and let go and let God and trust the process. This has been a difficult journey but it's definitely brought other parts of my life into perspective and the things I dwelled on before don't seem like such a big deal anymore. I refuse to be passive aggressive and I will not run or cower because I am a deserving woman who loves herself.

"God grant me the serenity to accept the things I cannot change, courage to change the things I can and wisdom to know the difference."

I waited for a few moments and then went back to see what kind of response I had received, and immediately started to cry from the number of people who were sharing their messages of support and love by posting directly on my update and through my inbox, and even by text and phone calls.

I was touched by that outpouring of love from women who shared their stories of what had happened to them, and elders who said thank you for doing what so many others have not been able to do.

I stayed up for another hour or so and read the messages, and then went to sleep knowing that I wasn't going to back down.

18

The next morning, I woke up and had breakfast and went and did my workout. I did a search online to see if there was a meeting I could get into before my mediation, but because I didn't know the addresses that well I reached out to a friend, Deborah, who I knew was also in recovery, and asked her if she could meet me.

I did not go to meetings easily and willingly most of the time, and often my godparents had to, and still have to, remind me it is important to my well-being. People find healing and sobriety in many ways, and different things work for different people. At that time in my life, they were such an important support and resource to have.

Deborah met me at a meeting that was only a block down from the mediation location. The meeting would end about half an hour before my mediation would begin. I listened to everyone share. There were people there in $5,000 suits and street people who had absolutely nothing but gratitude for life and their beautiful teachings to share. I felt blessed to be in the room that day.

As the meeting was coming to a close, the chairperson asked me to share. As always, I did so, because my mom told me if I was asked to share or talk I should never decline. She also told me whatever would come out was what needed to come out.

At the end of the meeting a few people approached me to offer their love and strength, and out of them all I remember one young woman named Veronica, who thanked me for what I was about to do. We exchanged names and still remain connected to this day. She reminds me of myself in all her thoughts and struggles. Her hug, her encouragement and her story reminded me why I was going through mediation and gave me strength that day. She, along with many other young women I've connected with, remind me why it is so important to share honestly and create safe spaces for women and girls.

With my hugs and prayers for strength and courage, I walked up the block to meet with the person who had stripped me of my personal power for the previous four months, wondering if he was even going to show up.

I walked into the lobby knowing I was a half an hour early and found a corner bench to sit down on. I opened up the message I had written the night before and there were new messages of support from over 100 people, as well as messages from people who were texting me and sending me love. They reminded me to pray; they reminded me to sing.

I sat there in the corner of that fancy hotel and I hummed the strong-woman song, held the rock and medicine that I had in my pocket, and when I finished I said a prayer. My hands and entire body were shaking and my lips were trembling. Everything felt very surreal and I again questioned whether he was going to be there. I knew what leadership dealt with on a daily basis; I knew that emergencies came up all the time; I knew that they were constantly being called away. I also knew that this man was at a high level of leadership where his schedule and presence at certain meetings was in even greater demand than a regular chief or leader.

My call with the mediator had done very little to make me feel confident, because I knew that he too was feeling overwhelmed with the man who was going to be sitting across from me. I could hear in his voice and language that he felt a little intimidated. I let the mediator know that his only job was to convey the message that I wanted to speak first without interruption.

I looked at my phone and saw that the time had come to walk back to the lobby to get on the elevator. It just so happened that as I was walking toward the elevators where everything had happened, he and the mediator were getting there at the same time.

I was a little shocked and surprised that he was there. I think the mediator felt as awkward as we did. We all said hello and stepped into the elevator together while I tried to find things to think about and stay grounded.

We stepped out of the elevator and walked toward the hotel room doubling as our meeting room, and I started paying attention to my breath. I thought about how strange it was to have a mediation like this, about sexual assault, in a hotel room.

The room we were in had a sitting area with two high-backed chairs and a couch. I chose to sit on the couch and the two men sat in the chairs. The mediator started by asking if we should get started, and then rambled about the purpose of the meeting and our agreements. Then the mediator looked at him and said that I wanted to start and that it was to be uninterrupted. I was shocked when his response was, "Of course. I would like to know what we are doing here."

The attention was then turned to me. I sat there for a minute and took a few breaths. I could feel the tears starting to come and I took a few more moments to breathe. I held the rock in my pocket in one hand and the medicine in the other.

I started off by telling him about my childhood. I told him all about growing up on the rez with an alcoholic mom and the sexual abuse I endured from the ages of four to ten. I then told him about my healing journey and my recovery and sobriety. I talked to him about the things I had gone through and how hard I had worked to be where I was.

Then I told him about the day he inappropriately touched me and hugged me. I told him how I felt when I left and how I felt when I woke up the next few mornings in fear. Then I told him about the chaos I went through because of his actions.

I told him that because I was abused as a child, I didn't understand boundaries and I even made excuses for him. I told him that there was a moment I wanted to drink, and I wanted to hurt myself because the memories and feelings that came up for me during and after the incident were so painful to process that I was having trouble coping.

As I finished sharing my story, I told him that I was there because I loved him and cared about him enough to tell him that what he was doing and how he was behaving wasn't good.

He broke down and cried.

He said that he knew how I felt and shared about his life and his experiences as a child. He expressed to me that he had really only meant to tell me how proud he was of me. He told me that he knew what I meant when I talked about boundaries and would do what he could to help make things right.

I let him know that I didn't want him to touch another woman like that again. At the time I believed the moment was sacred, ceremonial, and that change happened for the both of us. I believe in that moment he was honest about his intent not to hurt anyone, and we both made a commitment to support each other through the healing process.

For the first year I felt he was committed to his promise, but as time moved forward I think he truly convinced himself what had happened was misinterpreted in my eyes and he hadn't really done anything wrong.

We continue to see each other at meetings and gatherings but I no longer hold fear. I no longer feel stress and powerlessness.

That experience changed the way I carry and hold myself in all aspects of my life, and I am no longer afraid to speak up when I feel something is wrong. I don't say something every time, because it takes a lot of energy to address things like this properly and sometimes I am just too exhausted. While I don't call out every inappropriate action that I see, it is important to acknowledge that it still happens frequently and is still normalized in the way we do business and politics.

19

Over the next few months, I still struggled with vulnerability and kept my walls up. I didn't feel safe all the time but found myself more aware of my surroundings. I continued to work with companies who wanted to partner with and develop Indigenous communities and continued to build my consulting company that specialized in planning for communities.

My independent consulting company, Elaine Alec Consulting, was at a place where I was having a hard time keeping up. I was working twelve- to eighteen-hour days and travelling a lot, and I was starting to turn down opportunities. I also saw the opportunity to do some really meaningful work to change the way communities planned but knew that I couldn't do it alone.

I talked to my cousin Rosalie, our nation's lawyer, and told her I wanted to start a new company with the goal of eventually creating a planning firm composed of Indigenous planning experts. I knew many Indigenous planners doing really good work and many just needed the resources and training support to get out there and do the work.

She asked me if I would take on partners or associates to tackle this new undertaking and I realized I had honestly never considered it before. She told me it would be a good idea to think of people I knew and trusted who had skills and strengths in areas I didn't. She also told me to consider it like a marriage, that I would have to see myself in a lifelong relationship with them and ensure we had an exit plan in case things went bad, because divorces can get messy.

It didn't take me long to think of two individuals I trusted and wanted to spend more time with. They had skills and education and personalities that I admired, and I knew I could learn from them and we would grow together. I sent them both messages and asked if they wanted to meet for coffee to talk about the potential of working together.

I met with Chris Derickson, who was a council member and the CCP coordinator for the Westbank First Nation. He had a law degree and was currently working on his Master of Business. When I asked him if he would consider working with me as a partner or associate, he immediately said he wanted to be a partner. I was overwhelmed because I wasn't sure if either of them would even say yes.

A few days later I met with Jessie Hemphill, who had been on town council in Port Hardy and was the CCP coordinator for her nation, Gwa'sala-'Nakwaxda'xw. She had a masters in linguistics and was currently working on her masters in planning. She had been one of the first individuals I had reached out to when I began my position as the CCP coordinator in my community and she was quick to share everything she knew with me. She also let me know that she would be interested in becoming a partner in our company.

It was exciting and overwhelming to connect with two individuals I admired so much. We started setting up meetings to discuss our agreements and roles and responsibilities and how we wanted to work together.

We were dissatisfied with mainstream consulting models currently serving Indigenous communities and wanted to do business differently. We valued each other, family, community, culture and the land over profits, market share and growth. We were, and are, idealistic, yet we remain committed to our personal values and want to do our best to express them in a modern business environment.

We all agreed that we wanted to have a company that supported family first with an emphasis on personal wellness, allowing for a flexible work-life balance, including embracing the ability to bring kids to work and hiring family members as administrative support to work with us.

Early in our planning stages Jessie said she planned to have children, and I had a young daughter and wasn't sure if I would have any more kids, so when we discussed strengths and weaknesses we put pregnancy under a weakness, because we knew it would take us away from work. Chris immediately jumped up and said that children and family would not be viewed as a weakness or challenge to overcome, but a strength of having a majority of the company owned and operated by Indigenous women.

He didn't believe women should be penalized for taking time out to raise children; rather, they should be encouraged, supported and accepted as valuable contributing members of the team. He told us that family is not a hindrance but a human need that allows us to flourish in our personal and professional lives.

We all had a strong commitment to community, and we wanted to focus on building capacity in communities rather than creating a need for our services through focusing on training and sharing our intellectual property with our clients, with a goal of training the next generation of Indigenous planners.

On the environmental front, we wanted to maintain a small environmental footprint by foregoing traditional brick-and-mortar offices to reduce our reliance on traditional hard assets, and we wanted to maintain paperless offices.

We eventually settled on the name that Jessie brought forward from a friend: "Alderhill Planning Inc." Alderhill represents our last names: Alec, Derickson and Hemphill. We also gravitated toward the name because we learned that the alder tree plays a key role in healthy forest ecosystems, and it has the unique ability to convert atmospheric nitrogen into forms that can be used by other plants and add nutrients required for forests to grow. Alder trees are also known as "pioneer trees," able to mature under harsh conditions. They spread quickly and become rampant. We wanted to become a company of Indigenous planners supporting other Indigenous planners to reclaim spaces in their own communities and nations.

After a few months passed, and as I was working with Chris and Jessie to establish Alderhill, a group of individuals reached out to me to see if I was interested in joining their campaign team to support someone running for an Indigenous provincial leadership position. I thought it was a great opportunity and I believed in their platform, which supported community-driven work.

I went on the road to visit a few of the leaders whose votes this prospective provincial leader was trying to secure, and listened to the way he interacted with the voters. At the close of a meeting, he would ask for a commitment from the leaders for their vote in the upcoming election, and had papers ready for them to sign that would designate a proxy to vote on their behalf if they said they couldn't attend the election in person.

Based on our lists and numbers, I believe he went to visit 160 of the 203 First Nations communities in our province. I had never met anyone who worked as hard as this leader. In the end he ended up winning in the first ballot, which was almost unheard of. The leadership in B.C. totally supported his economic development agenda, and he asked me to stay on during his ninety-day transition as the chief of staff.

It was difficult for me to accept this position because I was in the middle of establishing a new company. I knew I was going to have to work long hours to get ahead of everything in order to properly support the new regional chief, who worked from five a.m. to eleven p.m. Anytime between those hours I could expect a phone call.

I attended meetings with provincial and federal leaders as well as our national Indigenous leaders. I started to see a pattern develop where they only worked with those who agreed with their agendas and anyone who opposed their work was shut out.

I was still learning about myself then, and I spent the majority of my time in that position stressed out and frustrated. I hadn't experienced stress knots in my shoulders until then. There was very little done to involve our people at the community level. Decisions were left up to people in Ottawa, who did the majority of their work with like-minded leadership and working groups made up of people who were hand-picked by the same crowd of people.

I stayed in that position until a new chief of staff was hired. I left to continue my work that brought me back into community, working in circles that brought together individuals who didn't always get along but knew that they shared the same vision and wanted to see a healthy community despite their differences.

I spent a lot of time going back and forth between my community work and the political circle, mostly because I was asked to advise chiefs on various issues that they were facing. Some of the leadership I worked with were very new and didn't know how to navigate their new position, so my advice to them was always to go into the community and talk to as many people as possible.

It wasn't long before controversy broke out with the regional chief I had supported. I stepped back from the issue for a number of reasons, but I was disappointed in his reaction to what had happened. In the beginning I took everything very personally, because I had stood up for him on so many occasions and put my social capital on the line for him. I eventually realized that everything I was feeling was a result of my ego and I let it go, realizing none of it had anything to do with me.

After some time had passed, I was again asked to help another of our leaders run in a provincial campaign. This time the candidate was a woman who was a hereditary chief from the Sto:lo, Chief Maureen Chapman. The experiences of supporting a woman in leadership and a man in leadership were so vastly different that I couldn't help but feel ill throughout the whole experience.

Unlike fundraising for a man, fundraising for her was difficult, because she didn't have a group of buddies to call up and get them to make calls and ask for favours, and she didn't make any promises to anyone. She was adamant that the money she received came from good sources.

She had also made commitments to her own nation that she wanted to make sure she kept before moving headfirst into campaign mode, so it took a little longer to sort out, but she was completely dedicated to doing everything in a good way.

She faced insults and comments from men, and people who supported her were attacked by the support teams of other candidates. Not only did we receive intimidating text messages, but some were sent to voting chiefs in an attempt to bully them into supporting their candidate.

There were a number of tactics used against our candidate, but she didn't worry too much about it herself. Instead, she focused on keeping her team in good spirits.

The day of the election was extremely draining. When they called the results from the first ballot, they tied 70–70. The most heartbreaking part about it was one of her supporters coming in two seconds after the ballot closed and realizing she had missed it. She lost the second ballot by four votes.

I went home and thought about it for a long time. I thought about the conversations we had with leadership and the support received from women to hold each other up in such a male-dominated realm, where many of our women were disregarded and ignored unless they understood the system and pushed their way in to be heard. We had very few women who were able to do that, and the ones that were had to have extremely powerful voices.

softened

I thought about the political and governance systems that we had adopted from colonial governments. I saw all the reasons why these foreign systems didn't work for us and how they continually divided us, repeatedly traumatizing individuals who didn't understand why things had to be so difficult.

After speaking out about my experience for approximately one year after I went through one of the roughest years of my life, I was elected as the Union of B.C. Indian Chiefs' Women's Representative. The position gave me the opportunity to find ways to create safe space for women and girls.

I spent the first year listening to women. I couldn't wrap my head around a role that didn't come with any instructions. I knew that the previous Women's Representative was heavily involved with the National Inquiry into Missing and Murdered Indigenous Women and Girls,[2] and I felt extremely intimidated because I had no idea how to be in that space, or if I even connected with the issues of MMIWG. I thought that I had no experience in dealing with the issues because I wasn't a direct family member of someone who had gone missing or been murdered. Later on, through my work, I realized that so many of us feel the same way and don't understand how we have all been affected, but many times it's just another thing to add to our long list of issues and fights.

I attended meetings and listened to families, and then listened to leadership debate how they would support the work. When I did speak I only had my own experience to share, and after every meeting women of all ages from Indigenous and non-Indigenous backgrounds would approach me and share their stories with me. By the end of the first year of my three-year term, over 200 women had disclosed and shared their stories with me about their communities and organizations.

I started to understand just how deeply trauma and violence affected every single individual in our communities and

---

[2] For more information on MMIWG, visit www.mmiwg-ffada.ca.

organizations. It didn't matter how well put together we looked or what position we held. We were all silently dealing with things that arose in our everyday lives and work, yet externally we all continued to try to move forward in hopes that the work we were doing was going to help improve the conditions for our people.

During this time, I met some of the most inspirational leaders across the province and Canada. I also had the opportunity to join another campaign for a woman from Northern Manitoba, who was the grand chief of thirty Northern Manitoba First Nations and running for our national organization. She was a long-standing advocate for Missing and Murdered Indigenous Women and Girls and created the hashtag #MMIW. She was also an accomplished businesswoman who knew how to occupy space in places where she might not be welcome.

As with my previous experience supporting a woman in politics, the next election I worked on was also to be a heartbreaking experience to witness. The bigger the arena is, the more brutal the politics become.

In anticipation of the upcoming national election, people started analyzing the political scene, the issues, the communities, the chiefs and the platforms. Typically at this stage, a campaign will review lists and determine where their support lies, look at the areas where they might need help getting influence, and then actively seek out people who have the influence they require. They see where they might need to split votes amongst weaker candidates, and they will have people run in specific areas just to split these votes and move their own candidates forward to the next ballot round.

Candidates make promises to leaders that they will move their projects or passions forward, and then they will often use fear-based tactics by saying that if the leaders don't support them, the other candidate won't have the skills or connections to help the leaders' causes. It can get really depressing for individuals with no experience in that atmosphere, or for those who refuse to play into those tactics, as they wonder if they can play the game without having any bargaining chips on the table.

In the end, it was difficult not to get caught up in the energy of the election. Looking back, there are so many things our team would have done differently to stay away from the theatrics. Even still, it was a sobering example of what is so wrong with the way our politics are run, at even the highest national level.

During the national election, I had a number of youth delegates and women who approached me at the annual assemblies and galas to disclose their experiences. They told me about their sexual harassment, assaults and rapes. They told me that they had approached their respective chiefs, regional chiefs, and even the national office to share their experiences and were dismissed.

We also received phone calls from the other candidates' teams who asked us to meet to discuss strategies for the next round of votes. Our team would wait for them and no one would show up, taking our time from meeting with chiefs and important caucus meetings. It wasn't until the election was over and we reflected on the experience that we realized we had fallen for diversion tactics.

After the election, I wrote an open letter to the national chief asking the Assembly of First Nations (AFN) to refrain from serving alcohol at their galas as one small way to create safe spaces for individuals at their meetings. They followed through in the first year at their December gala in 2017. My letter was never acknowledged, and since then they have gone back to serving alcohol. Women continue to be harassed and assaulted at AFN meetings with little to no acknowledgement. Many do not come forward because they don't believe that they will be listened to, and many are worried about their livelihoods.

I often think about all of the issues that our communities and organizations are going through, and the things that hold us back. It always comes back to a lack of trust and working from a fear-based system that promotes division and the picking of sides: right or wrong, good or bad.

As long as our Indigenous political organizations continue to work within colonial systems with board systems, society acts and voting structures that allow space for corruption, meaningful change will never occur and women will continue to be abused and disregarded as problems unless they play the game.

20

Around that time, I attended an Interior Region Health Caucus meeting in Kelowna. I ran into a woman named Crystal whom I had known from back home when I was a kid and used to babysit her daughter.

She mentioned to me that she was working for the Bonaparte community and I told her that was my dad's community. She said she was creating a community-based plan and wanted me to come work on it, so I gave her my information and told her she could connect with me anytime.

When I was younger, my mom would bring us to Bonaparte in the summer to spend time with my granny, my dad's mom, and we would spend time with our cousins and sometimes with my dad's other kids.

When I got older, I tried to go back and spend time with our family members who were a little older than me, but things had changed and there was a lot of drinking. I wasn't always welcomed with open arms, and one of my last visits there had left me crying. As I left the community, I stopped at my dad's grave and stood there for a moment. I told him that I loved him but that I didn't have any connection to his family and I wouldn't come back.

Throughout the years I attended meetings and gatherings, and whenever I introduced myself I always said who my parents and grandparents were and what land they had come from. I was always told to introduce myself that way so that people would know who I was and where I was from. I was also told that when

I introduced myself that way and said the names of my ancestors that it would call them into the room with me so that I was never alone.

So many times, after the gatherings and meetings, people would introduce themselves to me and tell me that they knew my dad. Sometimes they would be family, and sometimes they had worked in my dad's community and said that they wanted to invite me there to do some kind of work.

In the beginning, I was polite and never said that I held resentments toward members in my dad's family, but as I got older and started to understand myself and others I realized that I was hurt because I had felt rejected. Instead of admitting that, I continued to hold on to anger and resentment.

I realized that I did want to have a connection to my dad's family and community, because there was so much of him and his spirit that I connected with through those ties. But I found that whenever I got hurt I would get hard. That meant that whenever I was vulnerable and allowed myself to have feelings, it was so painful that it was easier for me to shut down and pretend that I didn't care anymore.

I went through a whole range of thoughts and emotions after running into the woman who ended up reconnecting me to my dad's community. I didn't really expect her to connect with me again, because I meet so many people who say they want to work with me but never end up calling.

A few weeks later, Crystal sent me a note and asked me to meet with her and one of the managers to talk about their goals. I spent the night in Kamloops and asked my friend Dave if we could connect while I was there and go to an AA meeting. I knew Dave through family ties and various support circles. I ended up having dinner with him and his wife and he asked me what I was doing there.

I let him know that I was going to Bonaparte the next day to talk about their health plan. He asked me if I had ever heard of

Ryan Day, a man who was from that community. I told him that I had never heard the last name Day from my dad's community but admitted that I didn't know many people from there.

He told me that he had been in a workshop with Ryan that day and that he was working for the Health Caucus, so I should connect with him because he might be able to help me with the work I was doing. I told him that I would reach out.

Later that night I checked out social media, found him and sent out a friend request. He immediately responded and let me know that he had heard I was going to be in the community but unfortunately wouldn't be there.

I was really nervous about visiting Bonaparte, and I wanted to make sure that I did extraordinary work that contributed to the community. I met a number of people who were really happy to see me, share stories with me and call me family. We did some really intense work on the first few visits that I made, and I connected deeply with a number of the staff members.

Over the next few weeks, Ryan stayed in touch with me through social media and we talked about my work and travel. It wasn't long after that when I happened to see an announcement on my newsfeed from a friend that Ryan had been elected chief of Bonaparte.

Bonaparte Indian Band is located just outside of Cache Creek, B.C. in Secwepemc territory, also known as the Shuswap. The term they use for leadership or chief is Kúkpi7.

I congratulated Kúkpi7 Ryan; I was excited to see so many young people elected into leadership positions and I knew that he had conducted home visits to talk to people and get to know them.

One of his first official duties was to welcome me and the chief from my community into his community. It was the first time we had met in person and I gave him a hug when he walked into the room. We were invited to do a presentation on comprehensive community planning and its importance in governance.

When we were done, he gifted us with canned huckleberries that he had picked and preserved himself. He was an exceptional host and a passionate speaker. He wanted to see the governance in his community shift to one that served the people.

As we got to know each other through social media, I paid attention to how much time he spent on the land. I thought he would be a great person to befriend and get out on the land with. Most of my conversations with individuals I worked with were kept strictly to networking over coffee or a meal, but I felt safe with Ryan and didn't worry about him becoming inappropriate with me. He was extremely intelligent, and sometimes intimidating because he used words I didn't understand.

He is five years younger than me. I was impressed with his outlook on life and how he listened. Not once did I think we had anything beyond a mutual friendship. I did know that he was considerate, trustworthy and dependable. On a few occasions, I wondered if I knew anyone I could introduce him to or set him up with.

There were moments when I wondered if he was flirting with me, but he was respectful of my space. He also knew what I had gone through with my sexual assault. I was open with him about the post-traumatic stress I was dealing with and the pressures I was under as a woman in the political and business arena. I told him I often had to share my ideas with men in leadership so they could bring it forward in order for others to hear it. At first I thought I had to explain to him what that meant, and he said very bluntly, "Oh, I am very well aware of my male privilege." At that moment I thought he was the coolest guy ever.

After spending a couple of occasions together and chatting through social media for two or three months, he asked me at our next meeting if he could take my hand. At first I thought he was going to show me something or read my palm. He started sharing a little bit, and I had a hard time figuring out what he was trying to say before he finally said he was interested in me.

It made me extremely uncomfortable, because it was the first time someone had given me a real choice of how to be in an intimate space like that. Although it was nothing more than him holding my hand between both of his, it felt so much more intimate to me than any other experience in my life.

No one had ever been respectful enough to ask to touch me first, and even after he told me his feelings there was no pressure to have any more physical contact with me. He was simply letting me know that he was interested in getting to know me better.

Until that point in my life, I had attracted and been attracted to people who had trust issues and their own unresolved trauma. I didn't think that I was deserving of someone who was good, because I truly believed that I was too damaged.

I had no problem telling him everything that I had been through and what I was still dealing with, and I thought that would be enough to stop him from pursuing anything with me.

I had no idea how to build a healthy relationship or accept love into my life. I had never been in a position where someone's only interest was to get to know me and to be in each other's space without pressure. There were so many times I felt comfortable about spending time with him, and then my inner dialogue would kick in and I would think of a million reasons why it wouldn't work. Most of it was because I was afraid of letting anyone know just how messed up I was. When times like that happened, I would act like I didn't care and talk about how busy I was and just didn't have time for a relationship.

He would tell me stories of his family and growing up. In my mind, I couldn't really imagine what it would be like to grow up in a home with both of my parents and all my siblings, to be cared for and taken care of and raised with each other even when they were all scattered across the country. He and his siblings had lost their dad before they became adults and their mom had raised them on her own. They graduated from high school, moved away and went to university. They all obtained degrees and were independent, but maintained relationships.

Self-respect and self-love were rooted into Ryan's whole being. He had so much confidence in the way he carried himself and had healthy boundaries of what he would accept into his life. If something didn't sound right to him, he wasn't afraid to question it. He didn't make decisions blindly and rarely took a person's word for anything.

It was the first time I was asked questions in a relationship. My opinions and ideas were often uncontested, and I could make statements without having to explain why I felt a certain way or why I did things the way I did. At first I had a hard time with this, wondering if he didn't trust me and my knowledge because I wasn't educated like he was.

Being around Ryan, even just in friendship, meant that having a relationship with him would mean complete accountability for me. There was no way I could blame him or put things on him unfairly. If I tried to spin a story for him to excuse myself for not showing up with 100 percent of myself, he would give me this amused look that always signalled to me that he was already going into his head to figure out if what I was saying was authentic.

It took months of spending time together, of questioning myself, of opening up a little and of working really hard on my self-defeating games to allow myself enough feelings to admit that I was falling in love with him.

To write that or even say it out loud was extremely difficult for me, because I wanted to be hardcore and I didn't want to give anyone any kind of control over me. I thought that falling in love meant that you had to give yourself away, which meant that the other person had something over you. Falling in love meant that hurt and disappointment would follow.

Allowing myself to be vulnerable was frightening and scary and messy. I didn't always enjoy the experience of falling in love. I had to deal with so much of my old belief systems about men, love and relationships and let them go in order to open myself up, and the process was uncomfortable.

Sometimes I would get lost in the moment and feel the feelings and the excitement and the happiness and love. In other moments I would feel something that would scare me or trigger me and then memories would come up that I had to constantly work through.

I started to realize that I wasn't as healed and healthy as I thought I was, and that drove me crazy because I couldn't turn around and blame anyone or deny it. I had to work through it by myself, and that was another excuse for me to stay out of a relationship.

I would explain that I still had a lot of work that I needed to do on myself, and that I needed to honour myself and take some time to work through it.

Ryan would challenge me and ask if being on my own would bring up the same emotions that I needed to work through, or if it would be the easy way because then I wouldn't have to work through some of my issues, which included trust, boundaries and self-love.

It was those moments when I would realize what I was doing in my head and understand that all of the fear and discomfort were being created solely by myself. My experiences in the past had caused me to create layers of protection. That protection included beliefs and rules that I made up so that I could survive the things I was going through at the time.

What I had to realize was those beliefs and rules made sense back then, but they were no longer relevant because I am no longer a helpless child. My walls and my protection and my beliefs may have protected me from getting hurt in the past when I was small, but as an adult they were keeping love away from me. My walls were keeping me from experiencing feelings, and not just the bad feelings of hurt and pain. They were also keeping me from true and pure love and joy.

It took months before I allowed my children to meet Ryan. Phoenix fell in love with him immediately. Although my daughter does love to meet new human beings in general, she was drawn to him and constantly tried to get him to carry her or cuddle her.

I started to meet his family, which were more scary moments for me. In the past, all of my experiences with families had caused me hurt and made me feel rejected. Because I tended to date people who had unresolved trauma, it meant they came from families that had unresolved trauma, and so interactions with them meant verbal, emotional or physical violence.

The first time I sat and had a meal with Ryan's family, I watched in awe at how they spoke and listened to each other. They looked and listened so lovingly and with so much care. They asked questions, but they didn't do it in a way that caused the other person to get defensive, which was what I was used to, which is why I had learned to never ask questions.

When I left them that day, I drove home and cried most of the way. I think I cried because it was so beautiful to witness that kind of love in a family. I had never really seen it before, except maybe on TV or in a movie. I think I cried because I felt like I couldn't see myself as part of a family like that. I felt like my presence would darken it and I didn't feel like I belonged.

By the time I got home I was crying because I was grateful, and I celebrated how far I had come in my life. I celebrated the hard work I had done to build a relationship with someone in such a beautiful way, and I allowed myself to be vulnerable enough to love myself and to feel deserving, loved and accepted.

Ryan and I got married in a traditional ceremony in the summer of 2017. We had our son Teslin Pelkamulaxw Alec in November 2017. The whole experience was another challenge of working through my own issues. I was forty years old, I had two other children with two other men, and I didn't know if I could handle another pregnancy.

There is not a day goes by that I don't stare at my husband and kids and give thanks for my life. I had never believed that this kind of life was possible for me, to have love, trust, respect and honesty in a relationship.

It is the first time in my life that I have felt safe and secure. I feel listened to and honoured, and I know I don't have to take care of everything and be all things. I have a safe place to fall and not be okay. There are times when my work or my emotions get to be overwhelming, and my husband Ryan is the place where I can cry and let go and feel taken care of.

He is the most amazing partner, companion and husband. He has never tried to fix me or tell me how to do things. I often tell him the reasons I love him, and he will tell me he has a hard time with some of them because all people should have the traits he has: decency, honesty and trustworthiness. It says a lot about him as a human being. His contribution to our family, to our communities, to our nation and to our lands has been tremendous. He does things in a very quiet and humble way, wishing he could do things without anyone knowing it was him.

We still work through our own issues, our loss and grief and pain, and do our best to not put our baggage on each other. We do our best to be accountable and own our self-defeating behaviours and honour each other for where we are at.

Our relationship seems to have just started, and yet we have already lived a lifetime of experiences together.

21

One thing I have learned in life and what I have had to accept is that healing is not something you achieve one day and then life is wonderful and perfect the next. I have spent so much time in my life feeling defeated and disappointed that I couldn't just get over things. I always wondered when the healing was going to stop so I could just live my life.

Sometimes I go through my day-to-day life without thinking about anything except what I need to get done. Other days it is a challenge for me to leave the house, respond to messages or go somewhere new.

So many things can trigger me and cause me to react, and for the most part I notice right away that I don't feel good. I can find ways to identify what it is and how I need to work through it so I can continue on with my day. I know that I have to do the hard work so that I can focus on being an individual that my family can count on.

I think many mainstream Canadians don't understand that we as Indigenous peoples have lifelong experiences of trauma and pain that we have to work through on a day-to-day basis. There is no understanding that we lack the privilege of not having experiences of trauma or racism.

What many people don't understand is that in addition to working through our own triggering on what is sometimes a daily basis, we also deal with having to balance a deep feeling of responsibility toward our families, communities and lands. We are often asked to put our feelings aside and let them go in order to help educate others or figure out ways to help them understand us better.

Almost every week something comes up for me and triggers a moment of regret and shame in how I have parented my children. I used to repeat to myself over and over again that I was a bad mom and that I did more damage than good to my son.

I really had no idea how to be a mom. I had Kyle when I was eighteen years old and then lost my mom to her stroke just before he turned one. By then his paternal grandmother had already taken him, because she told us that my mom and I both worked too much to take care of him and I didn't think I had a say in those decisions.

As the years passed and he would go back and forth between me and his grandparents, I would still drink and leave him with his stepdad, who also didn't know how to parent.

I had a short temper, didn't have rules, and often thought that I could leave him on his own by the age of ten because I had started being left when I was three years old. I remember comparing my life to my sons and thinking that I was doing better than my mom did and that helped me not feel so guilty at the time.

I had Phoenix when I was thirty-five. I had some years of sobriety and healing under my wing that helped me slow down from spending too much time at work. I had learned some patience and a little bit more about parenting, but I still struggled with being a mom because I didn't think I was great at it. Even if I was working, being a mom who could provide for her kids helped me to feel better about spending some time away. I knew that her dad loved spending time with her, and I could count on him to take care of her while I was away.

I was forty years old when I had Teslin with Ryan. Parenting with him has been an entirely new experience for me, because even though Teslin was Ryan's first child, he had a completely different understanding of what it meant to be a parent because of his upbringing and his mother's presence and love.

I would tell Ryan that I learned to be a woman and mother through Kyle. When Kyle would come home, he would see how I did things or didn't know how to do things, and he would tell me that "Grandma does it this way."

Back then I would brush it off or act like I didn't do it that way because I didn't want to. I acted like I didn't care because I was embarrassed and felt inferior as a woman. I felt I should know these things but I didn't.

As I went through the years, I really paid attention to what my adopted moms would share with me. My mom had brought these women into my life when I was younger, and they were always there to help me transition through some really difficult phases of my life. They continued to love and support me when I didn't love myself and they never judged me when I strayed off my path.

These last few years I have been open to learning and listening and paying attention. I was blessed to spend time with Ryan's mom Anne, who showed me what it was like to be loved and to love others with intention. She was constantly busy doing things and thinking of others, and she follows through on her plans and never makes excuses.

Anne's gentle way of doing things was passed on to her children and has made my husband one of the most loving and attentive fathers I have ever witnessed. He has shared with me his thoughts and beliefs about what he thinks is important when I am quick to brush things aside.

I have been able to follow through on schedules and commitments for my younger children. When I was younger I didn't do these things, because I was always afraid that I would disappoint someone or that I couldn't follow through because I didn't have the energy, money, transportation or know-how.

I didn't realize how important following through was for building my own self-esteem and perseverance. It has taken me practice and check-ins with myself to remind me what is important and to let myself parent with feelings and emotion.

There are times I will shut down when my kids want me all the time, whether it's needing cuddles or just being close. My first instinct used to be to push people away, because that's what happened to me when I was little. When people come into my space, I can't handle close contact for long periods of time before I will become overwhelmed.

During those times I catch myself and stop. I breathe to reset my mind and tell myself that my children need to be loved and cuddled. I used to beat myself up about that. I thought that if I was a good mother I should instinctively know to be warm and loving. I have learned to be easy on myself and know that I am doing the best I can with what I know.

On a few occasions when I have been multitasking motherhood and a career and my children are happy and thriving, I will take a moment to celebrate my victories and push past my guilt about wishing I could have been this kind of mother for my oldest son. He had to deal with a mom who knew nothing but drinking to hide the pain, and isolation from not being able to cuddle a mom who was in physical and emotional pain.

I know that Kyle has become the amazing young man he is because he was raised in his early years by his grandparents who nurtured him, spoke the language to him, and loved him so beautifully. Although I have done some things in my life that will forever stay with him, he has the courage to do the work he needs to move forward.

There have been times when I wanted to sit down with him and have some hard conversations to help me work through my own guilt. I have stopped myself because I know that when he needs to he will come to me to share what is on his mind. I have shared with him that I am always open to him being honest with me and will always do my best to provide a safe space for him to share. Over the years I have worked on building that trust with him.

There were many times when I wish I was more patient and loving, and hoped I had better instincts and warmth. There have been moments in my parenting when I have questioned my ability as a mother. My children have challenged me, and I have had to take moments to remember that they choose me to be their mother and have faith in my ability and teachings.

22

Our first stories talk about life before human beings were here, when Animal People roamed the earth and the land was different and had People Eaters.

When the Animal People were told that humans were coming, they would talk amongst themselves and ask, "What will we do for the People to Be?"

Each of our stories describes how we are to make decisions and what is important. From the moment we are born, we are welcomed into the world in a loving way. Our language is shared with us and our name is given. We are told who we are and where we come from, and our umbilical cord and placenta are taken care of to tie us to the land so that we always know that we belong to this place.

Our stories explain our laws and protocols for gathering. The story of the Four Food Chiefs told of how Chief Black Bear, Chief Spring Salmon, Chief Bitterroot and Chief Saskatoon Berry decided to prepare the world for the People to Be so that they had the best possible chance for survival.

Our stories imply that the People to Be are like children to the Animal People. All of our laws and stories centre around decision-making and how to make the world a safe place for the People to Be.

Later on in our stories, Sen'klip, or Coyote, was given powers by the Creator to transform the People Eaters so they could not harm the People to Be. One of our teachers once mentioned to me that everyone and everything has purpose. She talked about the presence of People Eaters in our stories, and she said that it was important to remember that Sen'klip didn't destroy them; instead he found ways to transform the People Eaters.

Where I come from, our teachings are not matriarchal but egalitarian. Our people had a belief system and teachings that told us that all beings have an equal role in this world. We understand that our systems were created to rely on each other and find ways to restore and regenerate.

Through my travels across different nations, many individuals have shared their stories and teachings with me. All of them carried the same values and principles of love-based teachings of respect and an understanding of purpose and roles within families and communities.

As I reflect back on my experiences, on what I understood and didn't understand at the time, I can see how it becomes easy to get caught up in the systems that uphold colonial structures.

When I attend meetings and see how we have adopted foreign governing systems, I see how these systems continue to hold us back. I hear people talk about *indigenizing* everything to make it ours, but what I witness is that our people are often handed something that was built and created from a patriarchal way of doing things.

When I go back to the community, I still see the division and fighting and the focus on who has more and who is being left behind and excluded.

Patriarchy is a system of society or government where men hold power and women are excluded from it. It is a system that promotes fear and sides being picking. It tells us that one group of people is wrong and needs to be converted, and it sets up systems that promote exclusion and shame.

Patriarchy lives in election systems and places where only certain people have a vote or a say. It lives in agendas that only allow for one topic to be discussed and where people have to obey the rules. It is a way of doing things that means people are often left out or left behind.

Patriarchy believes that emotion is weak and has no place in business or governance. It means leaving pieces of you behind when you sit at the table. It means that if you want to be part of the winning side, you have to comply and be ready to be a part of the team without holding them back.

Matriarchal and egalitarian systems promote love-based decision-making and space for people to share their emotions. Our teachings are shared with us from the moment we are born and evolve as we grow older. Our stories are told over and over again and repeated so that the teachings are embedded into our spirit, and every time we hear the stories we hear something different that helps us connect or learn something new.

It is because of this that we instinctively know what is wrong and what is right. We know that when we make good decisions we learn and grow. We also know that when we make bad decisions we have to deal with the consequences.

One story that illustrates this teaching concerns Coyote and his brother Fox. Fox was given the power to bring Coyote back to life. Coyote represents many lessons for our people, and his markings are left throughout our territories. He transformed the People Eaters into beings that were useful, and he transformed the land and waters so that they could sustain our people with food sources and places to gather.

There are also stories of when Coyote would get greedy and forget to do what he was told to ensure life was regenerated. When he became boastful, his powers were taken away from him.

I remember stories about him becoming boastful and wanting to show off or take more than he needed, and he would die. Fox would have to gather all of Coyote's bits that were scattered over the land. He would bring all the bits together, step over him four times and Coyote would come back to life.

My cousin Lauren Terbasket, who is also one of my teachers and mentors, told me that when I do work throughout the province and country I should remember to gather the bits. She said that in order to bring back life we have to gather up everything we can, all the pieces from different perspectives and experiences, and bring them all together. Sometimes it takes a long time and it seems like that time is wasted, but without all the bits we can't bring life back into the work we need to do.

While Fox can usually bring Coyote back to life, there is one story where Coyote does not come back: when he betrays his own daughter and is turned to rock. This was a very clear example to our people of the sacredness of our young women and the consequences of harming them.

23

Not only do our people work from a place of understanding the importance of all voices, we also understand that what we do affects everything else. We understand that we have to find ways to live in balance with everything around us in order to live sustainably.

When I began my work in community planning, I was taught the concept of nested systems. They remind me of teachings I learned when I travelled across the Prairies. I listened to a Cree medicine person talk about their system of putting children at the centre, surrounding them by elders, then by the women, and then by the men.

She spoke about how we all have roles in the community, and when enemies come to start a war we simply move systems and people in this way, and the roles remain intact.

She then talked about prophecies and one hundred years of darkness. She said that our ancestors knew what would happen. They knew our children would be taken and we would go through a time of suffering and a time of awakening.

She told us how our enemies found out that our children were the centre of our communities and so they took them from us. When that happened, our elders, women and men lost their roles within our communities, and our communities fell apart.

I heard stories from our relatives on Vancouver Island, who also talked about a nested system with the individual at the centre of the family, the community and the universe. They acknowledged that this balance went further than just the land—it involved the stars and beyond.

For my community, we also place the individual at the centre surrounded by family, community and land. However, in our language land is loosely translated as *tmxulaxw*, which talks about spirits, things you can see and cannot see, and a concrete knowledge that those things exist and that one thing cannot live without the other.

Residential school, colonization and patriarchy taught us many things, including shame, and that we were inferior and didn't matter in this world. It taught us that our ways of thinking, being and knowing were useless. It also taught us that caring for ourselves was selfish.

Since our communities have started to rebuild, we have tried to find ways to make things better. Back when Indian agents representing the Department of Indian Affairs first came to our communities, we were told how to do things. Our people were put on reserves with imaginary boundaries and told we were not allowed to leave unless we had permission or a permit. Water was diverted from our communities to service orchards and fields so settlers could make a living. Our creeks and rivers dried up and we were unable to grow much on the reserve.

I once heard a woman share that when our creek dried up the teachings stopped. She said it was the creek that provided the space for us to have sweat lodge and to tan hides and teach our young people about what they needed to do and what we needed to take care of.

Indian agents also used alcohol to bribe our people or to have documents signed to transfer land. It wasn't until the '70s that our people started to talk about asserting our right to govern ourselves.

At the time, many took to shutting down Department of Indian Affairs offices across the province. They wanted the federal government to give them the responsibility to manage their own affairs, and so the first band offices were created and certain responsibilities were transferred to administer federal government programs that were run by federal government dollars.

While it wasn't perfect we thought it was a win, and over the years we have learned that it has become yet another reason for our communities and nations to remain divided. We continue to live under fear-based thinking and compete with each other for government dollars. We wonder why one family has more than another, and who is taking the money and holding the rest of us down.

We have many helpers who work within the systems set in place by governments, working beyond eight hours a day. Many work six days a week and twelve to fourteen hours a day. Many of our people serve the community in various aspects and wear many different hats. These government dollars string small amounts of money along to create full-time jobs, but many times our well-intentioned people end up working eight different jobs in the community and become burned out.

Our leaders and our workers spend all this time focusing on ways to improve the conditions for our families, and our individuals worry about their children, cousins, uncles and grandparents, and put so much energy into fixing them or helping them.

We focus on the situation our communities are in through a lens of policy and process, seeing the divisions, the politics and how things are run. We spend all of our time trying to fix a broken system and make it our own.

As Indigenous peoples, we have always been told that we are a part of the land. We are the land. We speak for the land and have a great responsibility to protect it. We have spent generations fighting for our land to make sure that we take care of it for our future generations.

We do all this fighting and still wonder why things haven't changed. Things haven't changed for our people because we forgot about the most important piece of our system: the individual.

Because of residential schools, we were taught that we aren't important. We have spent a lifetime focusing on other people or causes that distract us from doing the work we need to do for ourselves.

The most important work we can do for our children is the kind we don't always want to do, the work that is vulnerable, the work that requires us to look at things we may have tried to hide because we didn't want to make a big deal about it or we didn't want people to judge us. We didn't want to make it look like we wanted pity.

A tradition of silence has become the norm for so many of our people. We don't talk about the hurt, the pain, the things that were done to us and the things we have done to other people, because we feel so much shame and this creates the silence. Silence has been killing our people. We carry the hurt inside and we try to hide it through numbing and forgetting with addictions to drinking, drugs, sex, love, gambling and working.

When we feed our addictions, we lose self-respect, self-love and trust for ourselves. Many times, we self-harm to punish ourselves because we think it will help the pain go away, instead of trying to find ways to forgive ourselves.

There are many individuals who are starting to speak out and share their stories. Every time someone shares their story they help erase the shame for others, and they don't feel so alone in their pain. Every time someone shares, they bring light to the darkness that cloaks our communities.

When people ask me, "How do I create and cultivate safe spaces?" I have a difficult time explaining it to them because it has been a long journey. It's a journey of understanding and embracing your story and sharing it with others. We can't expect others to share their stories, their hearts, their thoughts, and their truths if we are not willing to do the same.

One of the understandings our people had when making important decisions for planning and governance was the awareness that we all come to the circle with human experiences, perspectives, feelings and emotions, and these things need to be acknowledged and honoured before we are able to move on with the business at hand.

There are differences between our communities and nations, within our regions, and across the province. There are differences in how we do ceremony, pray and govern. I also believe we have shared values that resonate with many nations across North America.

As Indigenous peoples across the country have been tasked with working together to find solutions for our people, communities have made it clear that they want to remain autonomous and they want a process that supports communities to plan for themselves in a way that respects their distinctiveness.

Most of what I know was taught to me by elders in my community, and through the enowkinwixw process that was shared with me by Dr. Jeannette Armstrong, who has influenced academics throughout our nation. The enowkinwixw process supports the equality of voice within extremes of diversity; it sets protocols in place to empower and encourage different voices of community to contribute their views. I remember watching her translate for elders at our meetings. She was a young woman but spoke the language like my tema. My mom had all of her books and told me that Jeannette and her siblings had the minds of geniuses.

There have been a few moments when I have been questioned by individuals from other nations who did not want to participate in the enowkinwixw process because it wasn't from their nation.

Since then, I have learned to do protocol before leading a session. I will often reach out to elders and medicine people to make offerings and ask permission to speak my language and share stories from where I come from. I often take time to do prayers beforehand, acknowledging that I am a visitor and praying that what I share will be helpful and not harmful. I have learned to adapt the process by focusing on the cultivation of safe space through sharing a number of teachings from various nations. In each case, the common teaching is love.

I have done my best to help provide a variety of teachings and understanding through stories from my people, as well as through the teachings of others who have shared a common understanding that knowledge is meant to be shared. Take what you need and leave what you don't.

24

There are four necessary conditions required for cultivating safe space: understanding self, working from a love-based place, patience and discipline. These four conditions need to be understood before offering protocols to individuals, as this understanding will prepare them for important discussions ahead. They lay the foundation of how they will gather for the day.

The first condition and one of the hardest is understanding the self. Many times, we live in the past and hold on to ideas and beliefs that stop us from being open to others. When we have a strong understanding of self, it's easier for us to understand others and why they may act and speak the way they do. We often hear the saying that what bothers us or triggers us about others is something we need to address within ourselves. The first thing we do when we hear this is to become defensive and closed, especially if the person has some undesirable behaviours that we feel are the complete opposite of our own. When we understand ourselves, it's easier for us to be present when listening to others. It also makes it easier for us to stay out of our judgments and remain open to others' thoughts, ideas, perspectives and experiences.

The second condition is to work from a love-based place. In order to do this, it's important to love yourself and be comfortable with and embrace your character defects, to acknowledge your own story and be gentle on yourself. Working from a love-based place also means that you understand everyone has purpose in this life. Sometimes we don't agree with them or understand them, but we have faith that they are just as important.

Love-based emotions include love, hope, gratitude, faith, trust, confidence, forgiveness, self-love, compassion, respect and self-appreciation. Fear-based emotions include fear, anger, grief, shame, guilt, judgment, bitterness, frustration, doubt and insecurity. Much of how we do things today in governance and business arenas are based on fear.

In many ways, fear is easier because being controlled usually means you don't have to make decisions for yourself. It's easier to live in rules that others set for you, even if you don't like it. Living and working in fear-based conditions usually means that people are uncomfortable with emotion and run from it, hide from it, bury it or create conflicts and fights because it's easier than being vulnerable and dealing with the root of the problems.

Therefore, when creating love-based conditions it's important to set protocols in place so individuals can prepare themselves to get a little uncomfortable.

Patience is the next required condition, because once you begin working with a group of people with differing experiences and perspectives there will always be someone who doesn't follow protocols and agreements, or there are individuals who will come in after the protocols and agreements are made and not understand where everyone else is at. During times like these, I always find it helpful to reflect on the teachings of Fly, who reminds us that even a small and irritating voice must be respected.

Patience is the ability to remain calm and have tolerance when you're confronted with delays or trouble. Patience is usually easy to maintain when you already have a strong foundation of self-understanding, and love-based conditions are in place. It's also easier for other individuals in the circle to participate when everyone has the same understanding of the conditions laid out in the protocols or agreements.

The last condition required to cultivate safe space is discipline. In many cultures and beliefs, discipline is obtained through mentoring and lifelong learning. It is taught through stories, ceremony and spending time with elders.

In ceremony, there are high expectations for individuals to have discipline. There are times when conditions can be physically uncomfortable—it could be too hot or too cold, for example. There are times when the speaker, witness or host could have much to say and speak for a long period of time. In those cases, elders and teachers usually tell young people that they have to pay attention and take in everything they are hearing and do their best to sit still without fidgeting.

Paying attention is a discipline all on its own. It meant that you listen without interference from your own thoughts. We were taught to fully listen to the songs and prayers even if we didn't understand the language.

The last important part of discipline is the release of ego: the ability to listen without judgment and to listen without feeling the need to interrupt, teach or correct.

25

When it comes to making important decisions and governing, everyone must show up in their strongest and most authentic role, because that it is how they best contribute to the community.

Matriarchal and egalitarian systems honour every individual's purpose and role in the community. One of the steps to honouring everyone's role is to share and acknowledge the presence of differing perspectives and their importance.

There are a variety of examples of how to demonstrate personalities and perspective types, from Myers-Briggs to colour-based personalities. In our stories, we acknowledge four perspectives represented by each of the four food chiefs.

The four perspectives are the traditional, innovative, relationship and action perspectives.

The traditional perspectives represent the individuals who are connected to land. They remember how things have always been done and remind us of what is important. They are storytellers and language speakers, and they become our communities' and organizations' memory.

The innovative perspectives belong to the individuals who think outside the box. They look at systems and find ways to improve upon them and are creative in their thinking.

The relationship perspectives represent the ones who create workable systems and find ways to include everyone. They don't like leaving anyone behind, and often want to slow things down to include something or someone.

The action perspectives belong to the ones who provide security and like to get things done right away. They don't like talking too much about things and want to see things happen today.

Part of the challenge will be to understand that, even though individuals in the group have opposing perspectives, they are still important and still need to have a voice.

Often when in situations where decisions and plans are made, people organize groups of individuals who think like they do. They put together think tanks and committees of people who they work well with; they like the energy they have together and how quickly they are able to make decisions and move forward.

However, it is when they have completed their plan and presented it to everyone else that they run into trouble, because the other perspectives don't see themselves in the work and they have questions about how it was done and how the decisions were made. Many times, those excluded groups will feel angry, which usually stems from hurt because they've been shut out and feel unimportant.

The group who made the decisions doesn't always understand why everyone is trying to hold them back. They often feel proud of the work they have done, and when the rest of the people don't support the work they feel their ideas have been rejected.

Both groups of individuals don't understand that the experience they've just had was the result of following colonial systems that promote exclusion, shame and oppression.

In order to cultivate safe space for all individuals to participate in their ways of knowing and being, protocols and agreements are put in place in the enowkinwixw process so that individuals are able to speak about who they are and what is in their heart.

After individuals acknowledge the presence and importance of differing perspectives, they are then told to honour themselves for their ways of knowing and being. In order to show up and participate from their strongest and most important role, they have to be confident that it is a safe place to do so.

Time is spent validating everyone's perspectives and experiences, and the fact that each person thinks, hears and speaks in different ways. They understand the English language and terminology in different ways—some words offend while others are interpreted differently. Some people share their answers to questions through storytelling, while others want to keep everything brief, direct and to the point.

Some people may look at a question and not know how to answer it right away, and they might want you to interpret it to them in a way that they can understand. This is a good time to share with them that they can answer the question in whatever way they understand it because there is no right or wrong to how they see things.

Validating everyone in the circle and how they do things helps participants understand each other. It is an important part of the work so that the group can move forward with the same understanding.

In some teachings, ceremony and gatherings, being present at the same time is important for good governance. It is understood that when everyone has the same information we can make better decisions together. In some ceremony and gatherings, the door does not open again after it has been shut until the big work is done, because if people miss the protocols and agreements there is a chance they can misinterpret things and be unable to be proper witnesses. In some cases, if a family representative is known to be late to or miss important meetings or ceremony, they are replaced by someone else in the family to ensure all of the families are receiving the same information at the same time.

When cultivating a safe space, people understand there are often times when we cannot control certain situations and people may be late. However, when extending invitations for people to participate, let them know they are being invited because you value their perspective and that some of the work that will take place requires a commitment to being there on time and present for specific pieces.

Once protocols and sharing by each person in the circle is complete, it is okay to open up the space for people to come and go freely, providing them choice from that point on about how they want to participate.

Protocols and agreements are an acknowledgement of how people are going to be together and how they are going to honour each other. The following set of protocols is needed to hear what is in each other's hearts, so that everyone feels validated and heard. It is an acknowledgement that everyone is human, and keeping our emotions inside affects the way we might participate in decision-making. Decisions made from sadness, hurt or anger can cloud our thinking.

Four protocols for cultivating safe spaces:

1. **Promote Inclusion:** Every person in the circle will be given an opportunity to speak. Please do not interrupt the person speaking and please do your best to stay in the circle to listen to everyone's voice. Please do not debate, disagree or put down anyone's views. This protocol asks that we listen to and honour each other even if we don't agree with them. It asks that we do our best to honour everyone's purpose.

2. **Promote Validation:** Please practice active listening and witnessing. This can be the most challenging protocol, as it requires us to practice discipline and patience with each other. Some people may speak longer than we have asked, and some people may stray from why we are there. This

protocol asks that we do our best to listen to everything being said without thinking about what we want to say or letting our mind wander outside the room. It also asks that you do your best to stay open-minded without judging the other person's perspective and experience as right or wrong. This includes putting your phone or any other distractions away.

3. **Promote Well-Being:** Please take care of each other and practice self-care. Part of building community and trust is understanding that responsibility does not fall on one person, but rather the community or group as a whole. Please do not share personal information that individuals have shared in the circle.

4. **Promote Freedom:** Everyone has different experiences. Some people may be comfortable with protocols and sitting for long periods of time while others may have difficulty doing so for a variety of reasons, including health and dietary issues. This protocol also acknowledges that in order to have a space that is safe, people need to know they have choice. The protocols are put in place to help people make decisions and build trust and respect; they are not meant to make them uncomfortable or feel shame for not being able to participate in a way that is comfortable for everyone else.

28

As the decade has now come to a close as I write this, I reflect on what I've learned about individuals' desire to learn and connect with self.

A number of books were published by inspirational women this decade who motivated me to share my story, women like Michelle Obama and Arlene Dickinson. Nothing motivated me more this year than two new books that highlighted the strength of Indigenous women and inspired me to sit and write with discipline. Thank you to Helen Knott and Kristy Henkes-Joe.

The #MeToo movement brought awareness to the world. It let us know that we are not alone, and that harassment, violence and assault are no longer going to be hidden and protected. Although #MeToo brought much awareness to the mainstream population, it is still something that Indigenous communities hesitate to address.

This year, historic legislation came out in British Columbia which recognizes the United Nations Declaration on the Rights of Indigenous Peoples and our right to self-determination.[3] This work could not be possible without difficult and honest conversations between leadership in government and our Indigenous leadership.

Dr. Grand Chief Stewart Phillip referred to the experience as working through a marriage. It required trust and navigating

---

3   For more information on the United Nations Declaration on the Rights of Indigenous Peoples, visit www.un.org/development/desa/ indigenouspeoples/declaration-on-the-rights-of-indigenous-peoples.html

complicated differences. Our leadership acknowledged that it was our own differences that would keep us divided, and trust had to be built between our own leaders in order to sit across the table from government with a proactive and united front. Healing is not just needed at the individual level, it is needed at all levels of community, right into our leadership roles. One of our root words, *yil*, is used in leadership conversation and means "to bind together, to unify."

In the last decade, people across the country are only now beginning to learn about the traumas inflicted on Indigenous peoples from residential schools and the heartbreaking reality of Missing and Murdered Indigenous Women and Girls. It is not an Indigenous problem, it is the responsibility of each of us to take care of each other and strive to be unified and create balance. When one thing is unbalanced, it affects all things.

Canadians continue to ask the questions, "How does this happen?" and "What can we do?"

I have wanted to write a book since I was ten years old when my elementary school teacher told me I should be a writer, and it has stuck with me throughout my life. It was the one goal I was afraid to strive for and I sat down for years trying to get started, but it was never the right time.

Writing is deeply personal, and I always worried that I wasn't good enough. I was scared of working hard and then facing rejection. I used to be ashamed that I couldn't finish school. Now I proudly share what I know all across this country because everything I know and am comes from Indigenous teachings and ways of knowing and being.

One of my beautiful friends, Anne Bérubé, told me that "creativity lives on the lips of vulnerability," and in this life, vulnerability has been one of the most frightening places for me to go.

In my twenty years of working in Indigenous communities across Canada and with various governments as a community planner, I am often asked, "How do we promote healing, and how do we cultivate and create safe spaces for individuals to have difficult conversations? Why can't we just get over it and move forward? What is holding us back?"

It is a question I haven't been able to answer in a way people want to hear, because the answer always brings us back to individual healing and reconciliation. We cannot change or heal what we do not acknowledge, but it is a place not many people want to go.

This has been a difficult book to write. I had to work through remembering things I didn't want to remember. I wanted to acknowledge my life honestly about growing up as the oldest child of an alcoholic, but I also wanted to make sure that people understood the beauty, teachings and love that my mom brought into the world.

My mom passed away two years ago, when I was pregnant with Teslin. She lived for twenty years in a care home while unable to speak, and yet was still able to teach us so much. She too wanted to write a book, and I did my best to capture the things she shared with me. I am the woman I am today because I chose her to be my mom.